ACCLAIM FOR
SPIRITUALITY 101

SPIRITUALITY 101

FOR THE DROPOUTS OF THE SCHOOL OF LIFE

(A REVIEW FOR THE FINAL EXAM)

IVÁN FIGUEROA OTERO, MD

BALBOA.
PRESS
A DIVISION OF HAY HOUSE

CREDITS

Author: Ivan Figueroa Otero, MD
Editor: Yasmin Rodriguez
Cover Design and Graphic Art: GA Design
Photography: Dr. Figueroa: Emmanuel Berrios

Balboa Press books may be ordered through booksellers or by contacting:

Balboa Press
A Division of Hay House
1663 Liberty Drive
Bloomington, IN 47403
www.balboapress.com
1 (877) 407-4847

Print information available on the last page.

ISBN: 978-1-5043-4675-7 (sc)
ISBN: 978-1-5043-4678-8 (e)

Balboa Press rev. date: 12/21/2015

ABOUT THE COVER IMAGE: FRACTALS

Fractals are mathematical sets of repetitive geometrical shapes. A lot of natural structures are fractals, since there is a tendency in nature to repeat mathematical and geometrical sequences. For me, the repetition of structures of the macrocosm (the world of the big things) in the microcosm (the world of the little things) seems to establish a common (holographic) thread between all parts of the universe, as described in the book.

DEDICATION

I dedicate this book to all the teachers and students who have been my classmates in the School of Life, and who inspired me to share all their experiences and lessons. Without them, I would not have progressed in this School.

If you think of this book as a mirror, and you see yourself in its reflection, please share the merit for the knowledge gathered from its pages.

CONTENTS

ACKNOWLEDGEMENTS

Among the travelers who have shared this endless journey, I want to give special thanks to my children, their mother, and my patient wife Ivette, who so lovingly supported my crazy old ways.

I also want to thank my spiritual guides, Masters of the Nyingma tradition of Tibetan Buddhist, the Venerable Khenchen Palden Sherab Rinpoche and Khenpo Tsewang Dongyal Rinpoche, from which I learned much of the training of the mind that I describe in this book.

Finally, my thanks to my mother, Doña Berta, for the hours spent reading the Christian Bible to me during my childhood, with the assurance that it would someday offer me strength through the difficult moments of my life.

"The Master is nothing but a disciple who would like to help others find their mastery"

"The weapons of a true Warrior of Light are compassion and patience to wait for others to learn what he learned"

—**Ivan Figueroa Otero MD**

SOLITUDE

Solitude is a conceptual, not a situational, state.
It is the psychic deprivation or alienation
of love's primordial nature
potentially residing in every sentient
being within our universe.
Yet, it still exists within the clamorous
effervescence of crowds.
As in a magical paradox, this feeling of
isolation disappears spontaneously
when we enter the solace of our inner silence,
which makes us feel nurtured and satiated
by the pure essence of Love.

After you try this indescribable delicacy,
there comes a new way to look at the infinite and variable
manifestations of apparent reality,
that allows us to observe them without judging
their illusory purposes and results.
This new vision, born of our hearts and
from all beings among our universe,
dissolves all traces of suffering away from ourselves
when we realize Happiness has always been within us on this
timeless path.

Ivan Figueroa Otero

INTRODUCTION

"DROPOUTS OF TRADITIONAL SCHOOLS" VS. *DROPOUTS OF THE SCHOOL OF LIFE*

In traditional schools, a "dropout" is a person who usually has flunked his exams and left school. But in the School Of Life, flunking doesn't mean failing. It's more like a learning experience that began at some moment and that hasn't been completed yet, since the options for repeating the lesson never run out.

In the School Of Life there are no grades or organized curriculum. Everyone comes to learn and progress in specific areas, and your lessons are structured by your daily life. It's as if the curriculum were created while you learn. Each experience is a new opportunity to grow and develop as whole beings, and everyone decides when he or she has learned sufficiently to move on to the next course.

Who, then, are the *dropouts* in the School Of Life? They're the ones that don't feel satisfied with their lives. Those who, for some reason, are unhappy, stressed, insecure, sad or angry may feel they have *flunked* some subject in their personal progress. In those cases, the experiences will be repeated until the blockage is overcome in order to continue progressing.

Fully graduating from the School Of Life is a human being's most important process. The thing is, in that process exams are administered on a same-day basis, just as the class! That's why when we flunk, things get harder, because next day's exam will include the material from the previous one. People who flunk without realizing that they can retake the exam, are boycotting themselves when they stop trying to pass it.

I'm one of those life *dropouts*, having repeated many subjects and during that experience, I have learned a bit about how to facilitate the test-passing process (tests which are about overcoming life experiences). This book is one of many that are coming out to help *dropouts*, and should not be construed as the only way to progress in life.

As in every school, in the School Of Life there are levels corresponding to our awakening to the experience of living. In this school, the teachers are the very same students that have passed yesterday's subjects. This educational system is like an infinite hierarchy comprised by levels, where the person placed lowest learns from the one a little higher than himself, and the latter teaches the next person in descending order.

If the School Of Life is full of *dropouts*, as is happening nowadays, alumni from advanced levels return and share their acquired wisdom cumulatively with large groups in lower levels, to help them pass the corresponding exams. These dropouts perhaps were the ones Jesus referred to when he said: "the poor in Spirit". They're also the same ones He was referencing when He said, "Forgive them, for they know not what they do."

The topics covered in this review constitute my experience on how I interpreted life's lessons in class, and how these could guide others in their respective paths along the School Of Life's infinite chain.

I want to express my deepest gratitude to all those who became my Teachers at every stage of my journey and who helped me to better understand my lessons of life. My heartfelt apologies to those whom, because of my lack of awareness, I caused any discomfort during my learning process.

I should point out this is not a book about religion, but of spirituality, and I will explain the difference through its contents. I will use tools from different religions to facilitate the understanding of spiritual concepts that unite religions rather than separate them. I hope this book will become one of many ways in which Life prepares us to enjoy universal Love.

Hopefully by the end of this book you will all be able have your own answers to life's archetypal questions: Who am I? Where do I come from? Where do I go from here? And that, as in the included poem, you will find out that the origins of Happiness have never left our side since the beginning of our common and infinite cosmic experience. Let's start this lesson of Love with a joyful heart.

Ivan Figueroa Otero MD

EXPLANATION OF SYMBOLS

	When you apply this you get a star.
	A question that will surely be in the exam. Phrases to study and to apply reason (brain's left hemisphere).
	Phrases to meditate and use the heart (brain's right hemisphere).
	Selfish attitude or action that generates unease or suffering in the person and those around him or her.

CHAPTER I

THE ORIGIN OF THE UNIVERSE

(How did we ever get into this mess?)

This chapter's main lesson focuses on answering the questions human beings ask themselves at some point in their lives: Who Am I? Where do I come from? Where am I going? To understand this, we have to carefully tread into the realm of science. Don't be afraid, since I'll lead you by the hand the whole way.

Glossary, Chapter I

The Big Bang—This is the scientific community's mainstream hypothesis to explain the origin of our universe. It proposes that the universe originated from a point of massive denseness or singularity, where nothing existed before, but whence everything would emerge from (logical, isn't it?). Don't feel bad if you didn't understand, since not even the experts agree on this! From this silent explosion, progressively and expansively, our Universe manifested itself in all of its magnificent splendor. Since that moment, many scientists' minds have crashed like overloaded computers trying to understand this phenomenon!

Antimatter—The opposite of matter, which science postulates existed in equal amounts with matter after the Big Bang, but which scientists have lost track of since then. It is believed to give rise to matter but they don't know how (you see how crystal clear and precise science is?). At present, antimatter is nearly undetectable by our instruments' scientific measurements.

Dark Energy—An energy known to exist due to the influence it exerts upon matter, occupying a large portion of space in the universe (72%), but which has never been seen or measured (I won't go on or I'll trip up!).

Dark Matter—That which occupies the other 23% of the Universe, though we know nothing about it, save for its influence upon gravity.

Matter—That which constitutes our understandable, measurable and visible universe, being the 5% in which we live (???).

Hologram—Tridimensional projection obtained from a flat image, by means of laser ray techniques. It is presently being used in television to transmit a person's image to faraway places. We soon shall be seeing this technology in our homes. The important thing is to understand that a scientist, Dr. Bhom, established that from any part of an object in the universe, the original can be completely replicated. This suggests that the information of the complete image is stored in each of its parts, and that there is an inherent form of communication among all of them.

Dimension—The way we perceive our conscience as being within space (3 dimensions, width, length and depth or height), plus the perception of time. This way of observing the universe is not the same for all animals. For example, ants only see 2 dimensions and do not perceive height (is that why they don't fall off walls?). The quality of being able to observe a tridimensional universe depends on our binocular vision and the way in which our brain processes it. When we lose sight in one eye we lose tridimensional vision, but not that of the other senses (if we don't keep our distance from other objects, we will definitely bump into them and feel it in our body, and the blind can read the tridimensional shapes of Braille with their fingers).

Time—It's a very subjective definition of the observer's experience when he or she interprets a series of events with the 5 senses and, based on memory's cerebral capacity, divides them into imaginary segments of the present, the past and the future. To establish time, we use references based on the seasons' observable changes (climates) and the cycles of day and night. Based on these changes, mankind has divided time into sections comprising seconds, minutes, hours, days, months, years, centuries, etc. (now you understand why it's so difficult to be on time for appointments!!!).

Einstein's theory of relativity of time—Clarifies scientifically that time will be interpreted differently from location to location in the Universe. It establishes that the maximum speed that a particle or material object can attain in the universe is the speed of light, and the faster the particle travels, the slower will the passage of time and of aging in the particle be experienced. This would imply that when a particle reaches the speed of light, its time stops and it disappears for us in our tridimensional time (remember this, because we will make reference to it later.)

Love—Potential state that cannot be measured scientifically, from which all possibilities of manifestation exists, and from which life originates, as well as the conscience to perceive it in all of its infinite and contrasting manifestations. It's the light and the sound that existed before the Big Bang, the same way these rest in the night before sunrise. Its nature is infinite patience, equanimity, understanding and tolerance, which allows its children the free will of how to use it. This nature unites each part of creation into a web or tapestry, woven by the unbreakable force of Love (I am what I am). (And where did romance go?)

And in the beginning only Love existed. And in its dream it saw all the possibilities of Creation, and a great explosion woke it, and upon opening her eyes she was no longer alone! (if you don't understand this, you must be men!).

Due to the discrepancies in all the accounts of the creation of the universe found in our history's main religions, and because of my lack of knowledge of them, I have chosen to focus my discussion in the information science has supplied us and my interpretation of this vision.

It's interesting to share with you (as you will see later) that my study of this scientific vision of the universe, and of

Buddhism's cosmological vision, is what once again brought me closer to my Christian roots. You must understand that the study of other religious approaches helped me to better comprehend those of my upbringing.

The most accepted theory for the formation of the universe is that of the Big Bang, which posits that everything arose from a single point or singularity where it was in a potential state, as a great explosion, which created a continually expanding universe. Initially, this universe was made up in equal parts of matter (50% - what we see and believe we are) and antimatter (50% - what we don't see and don't know what it is). In some mysterious way, antimatter was reduced to a negligible amount that couldn't be measured, that we know now exists but we can't perceive it, and later two new components cropped up: dark energy (72%) and dark matter (23%) that may be the measurable manifestation of antimatter. If we add 72% + 23% = 95%, it tells us that the universe we live in is only 5% of the total! (wow, and where the heck is all of that which seems to surrounds us?).

We're only aware of 5% of our universe (Is that why there are so many alienated people in this planet?).

This creates a paradox for us: it seems we have been deceived by the assumption that man is the center of this universe and the crowning achievement of creation! (Don't be afraid. Later I'll give you information that will increase your self-esteem again). And why is it that we don't perceive the rest of our existent universe? To try to understand this better, we must divide our universe into two great parts: one which can be perceived and another which cannot be perceived by our 5 senses: sight, touch, smell, hearing and taste.

We must point out that the abilities regarding these senses vary from animal to animal. And those of some animals (yes, we're animals, some a bit more than others!) are superior or inferior to ours, which implies that though we share the same universe, we don't perceive the same perspective of it. Our consciousness of the universe is the sum of the experiences that we have lived through, with all the senses plus the interpretation we have learned during our process of socialization, upbringing, education and hereditary tendencies. This implies that our personality resembles programming (software) influenced by what we have learned in our life and our parents' hereditary traits (later we'll go into more detail on this, in other chapters).

 Our universe is like the moon's reflection upon a lake.

Let's imagine a primitive being, when he observed the moon's reflection upon a quiet body of water for the first time, and that he was not aware of the image's origin. That's the same way we observe (erroneously) that our universe constitutes the totality of itself, when our 5 senses only allow us to see less than 5% of the total. We live in a material universe, which is a hologram of the totality of the universe, and participate in a limited perception of our reality. This holographic image is a tridimensional illusion which, along with the relative vision of time, imprisons us in its fantasy of birth and death that makes us feel the fear and the suffering, and does not let us perceive our true origin.

This image of the universe is like a majestic play where we participate in many roles and scripts, where, when we meet later with our fellow actors in the café, we only talk about the quality of the acting and how we could improve it for the next play, but not about the prominence of each individual role.

To find our origin we must look to the stars and the original explosion, and not the image reflected in the lake created by our 5 senses (not all that glitters is gold! Beware the wolf in sheep's clothing! [appearances are deceiving]).

Are we sons of Love (God) or are we sons of man?

Scientifically, as Carl Sagan said, we are children of the stars since we are made up of cosmic dust that originated after the Big Bang. This scientific fact makes us bearers of a common lineage that later gave birth to DNA, the hereditary material that originated life on our planet.

> No matter our race, color or sex, we all come from that first DNA. But if we had already established that matter had manifested in only 5% of our reality, and that the rest of the universe (the other 95%) had originated in the same place, we must conclude that this part too belongs to our common lineage. This seems to imply that our origin is of a dual nature, where we are sons of Love (God-antimatter) as well as we are sons of man (matter-time).

If we understand that the biological DNA has chronicled within it the memory of all that has happened in our matter since the Big Bang, we would have to accept that the rest of the 95% of the universe, antimatter, etc., also must have a memory or recording of an anti-material (Spiritual) DNA, of whose lineage (kinship) we would also participate. For now, just accept that we are beings of a dual manifestation, as sons of God and sons of man, with a common lineage irrespective of race, sex or religion.

Science also polarizes the universe into two parts according to its scientific explanation: Newton's laws, which defined the behavior of material objects on a large scale, and quantum [physics], which defines the laws of behavior on smaller scales such as those of subatomic particles. In the former, 2 + 2 always equals 4, but in the latter, 4 is only one of many probabilities. In quantum physics, nothing is impossible – only more or less improbable. The observer influences the manifestation of the observed with his thoughts.

Do you then understand the importance of our thought's intent? Look at the table on the following page.

CLASSIC PHYSICS	QUANTUM PHYSICS
(Material Universe - 5%) (The Self as a Son of Man)	(Antimatter Universe - 95%) (The Self as a Son of Love - God)
It's deterministic: If we know an object's position and velocity, we can determine where it is going.	It's probabilistic: You can never know with absolute certainty what something will concretely turn into. It cannot be reproduced since it varies depending on the interpretation of the observer.

It's reductionist: The parts of this universe seem to act independently from others.	It's holistic: The Universe is a unified holographic whole, whose parts instantaneously interact with each other.
The observer observes the Universe as something outside himself and does not feel a part of it. Reality is external and independent of the observer.	The observer is an interdependent part of his universe. He is a microcosm of his macrocosm, and maintains a holographic relationship with the whole. The universe surrounding him can be changed with his thought intent.
It's applicable to the world on a large scale, but not to the subatomic world.	Applicable to every scale in the universe, since everything at a large scale is composed of subatomic particles.
It's based on the knowledge of "absolute truths or laws" Time is absolute every place in the universe. The universe is tridimensional.	It's based on the knowledge of a universe that changes continually in infinite cycles with "tendencies to exist" or "tendencies to happen". Time is relative everyplace in the universe, according to the object's and the observer's velocity (law of time relativity). The universe is multidimensional.

The development of modern science was particularly influenced by the dual concept of self postulated by Cartesian theory where, using Isaac Newton's mechanical theory of physics, it was stated that "I think, therefore I am". Here the knowledge and study process had to limit itself to the world of rational and scientific analysis based on laws established through the use of the 5 senses (if I don't perceive it, it doesn't exist). This part, man's material part, seemed to be independent of the one that existed beyond the physical, what man termed metaphysics – something that cannot be measured and unknowable according to scientific laws. Metaphysics lay outside the realm of reason to study it. This created a mechanical vision of human beings where the metaphysical (spirit) or transcendental had no importance nor influence over the material part.

This vision prevailed until the development of quantum physics and Einstein's theory of relativity at the beginning of the 20th century. These new theories began to document the existence of a subatomic universe, invisible, outside absolute time, and the existence of dimensions beyond the three traditional ones we perceive (this created a scientific "free-for-all" that hasn't ended yet). For the first time, the metaphysical or transcendental (antimatter) and multidimensional was established as a reality in our physical universe. Based on this new knowledge, I postulate that we should change the Cartesian axiom to "I am, therefore I think". I say this because after the Big Bang, matter originated from antimatter, which in turn originated from an indefinable point that I define as Love.

This position is reinforced in one of the few times in the Bible that God describes himself when, at Mount Sinai, at Moses' insistence (in one of the many translated versions) He replies, "I am that I am" and "I am what I am". This reflects the indefinable and inclusive nature of His greatness, that lovingly adjusts to what his children want Him to be for them, that was the primordial state of everything before the Big Bang. We can then infer that we (men and women) are, in the manifestation of matter, The Son/Daughter of Man ("I am who I am") (revise the term "Love").

Summing up, the universe originates from a point (singularity) where, due to a large explosion of Love (God), it initially manifests itself in infinite forms (Spirit, Son of God, antimatter, dark matter, dark energy) and these in turn manifest in the self's dual form (The Son of God within the son of Man, The Christ) forming the Universal trinity =

**GOD
(LOVE)
(SINGULARITY)**

**SON OF GOD
(SPIRIT - ANTIMATTER)**

**SON OF GOD WITHIN THE SON OF MAN
(DUAL MANIFESTATION OF ANTIMATTER
WITHIN MATTER)**

Co-responsibility and co-creation are the two qualities that should guide us in sharing this universe

In order to understand these concepts, we must review what we have previously explained. When we define our universe as holographic and quantic, we must remember that the whole universe is interconnected by means of the inexorable matrix that unites it in Love, since each part belongs to the same family or lineage, no matter how distant of different we perceive ourselves in the material planes of time and space. An action happening in a part of the quantic hologram impacts all parts of the hologram. Remember the Biblical quotes, "Just as you do for smallest of my brothers, you do unto Me", "Love thy neighbor as thyself".

This seems to confirm the common lineage of the universe and all of its parts. From this realization of being a part of a great universal family and from the golden rule, "Do not do unto others what you would not want done to yourself," arises the awareness of co-responsibility for our actions. Later, in another chapter, I shall explain how the law of Love corrects imbalances originated by the irresponsible actions of its children.

Co-creation arises with the Self's (observer) ability to perceive the Universe in all of the infinite possibilities that the hologram offers, allowing it – according to its individual perspective or vision – to interpret (like in Clint Eastwood's movie) The good, The bad, The ugly, and The beautiful.

This critical way of seeing the universe limits the material self (Son of Man) who is not aware that the is also a Son of God (quantum self) and that he lives imprisoned in his jail (selfishness) with the bars created by his own 5 senses. We already know that this mental action in the quantic holographic world alters the surrounding universe, creating an imbalance throughout the hologram. This imbalance is what we have co-created co-responsibly by our lack of mental awareness of its effect on the rest of the universe.

That's why the intention of how we want to observe our universe must always be based in the common lineage of Love.

This must make us aware that the only way in which Love can manifest in the universe is by means of the Sons of Man, manifesting the spiritual nature, or the Son of God (the Christ).

Now let's answers the first two questions that began our chapter.

Where do I come from?

We are the children of the Great Explosion of Love that begot the whole Universe. We bear a common lineage that unites us in its interminable matrix, that is manifested in all of the different and infinite dimensions, allowing us to participate in this unending co-creation with an attitude of loving co-responsibility.

Who am I?

I am a being of light (Love), with innumerable dimensional manifestations of shadings of Love and Life. The transitory experience within matter, time and space (human being) resides in those manifestations. This allows me the use of my free will in a co-responsible way in the co-creative process of life.

Now you understand why we can't blame others for our failures and suffering?

Homework

Exercise to find the other 95% of our universe.

1) Let's observe everything that surrounds us with our 5 senses. Can we see, smell, feel, hear and taste everything that exists? We know we can't. Let's think about the things we know exist but we can't perceive them. Have we ever seen the wind that moves a tree's branches? Has anyone seen or felt X-rays when they're taken or seen or felt the infinite emissions of the sun's rays, which bombard us and penetrate our bodies?

Have we ever seen the incessant thoughts that our minds generate? Can anyone tell us precisely where the mind is and describe its configuration? Can anyone see and locate where our emotions happen? Do we see all of the millions of microscopic and submicroscopic organisms that live throughout the surface of our bodies? Gazing at the body externally, we can't see all the types of cells that constitute all of our organs. No one doubts most of the preceding things, but no one has ever seen them without special instruments.

These simple observations make us realize that not everything that exists is perceivable, and that perceivable things are not the only ones that exist. Are you already finding where the rest of the universe is?

2) Look around you and note everything that you see, and search for its origin. Discover if you can see, smell, touch, taste or hear your thoughts or those of other persons. Try to see or hear the electrical currents that create the nerve conduction of those thoughts. Feel the surface of your bodies and that of objects surrounding you. Observe their texture, solidity and elasticity. See your hands and understand that they are made of muscular tissue, cartilage and bone, which in turn is composed of invisible cells, of molecules and organic compounds and, in the last instance, is made out of invisible subatomic particles.

3) All of the other parts of your body are made up of the same elementary particles. But why do we see them so differently? How did we learn to differentiate our universe? The names granted to these qualities are the same in every language?

Observe how, during your lives, your actions have influenced other persons, your environment and your current situation.

4) Finally, meditate silently about what you have observed and answer yourselves: Where's my visible self or individuality? Where's my invisible part? If you find it, send me an e-mail and tell me where you found it!

Bonus questions to improve your grade (10 points/ question for bookworms)

1) If the Big Bang sprang from a singularity where everything not yet manifested was still in a potential condensed state, where did the preexisting come from?

2) Why do I say that the explosion was silent?

3) Why do I refer to Love as feminine? (Study the theory of Yin and Yang)

4) Why, if we are all children of God, created in His image and likeness, not all of us manifest the Love in the universe? Check Jesus' phrase during his last moments, "Forgive them, Father, for they know not what they do." And we could add, "Because they have forgotten that they are your sons and my brothers in Spirit".

5) If, at every moment, the process of interpreting, understanding, investigating and reasoning only takes place with less than 5% of the data, can anyone affirm that he possesses absolute truth or is completely right? What position must we assume when we disagree with others regarding the way life should be understood?

How many possible visions can exist of what God means to man?

CHAPTER II

AS RIVERS OF THE GREAT OCEAN

The false perception of individualism and separation.

"The Universe is like a great ocean of Qi in which we are as rivers that drain into it. In a given moment, we may believe that we are only individual rivers, but when we join it, we realize that we were never separated from the ocean. Some of us emerge as wide and turbulent rivers. Others, as tranquil or as weak streams, but we're never alone in our path. Whatever affects the ocean, affects the river and what affects the river, impacts the ocean."
— Iván Figueroa Otero MD

Glossary, Chapter II

The Law of Conservation of Energy—The first law of Thermodynamics, that affirms that energy cannot be created or destroyed, it can only be transformed from one form to another. Ex. Energy ⟷ matter in bidirectional infinite form.

It seems like this universe will never end?

Qi or Chi—Term used in the Chinese Oriental medical tradition to refer to energy that may be in higher vibratory states (energy) or lower or denser ones (matter).

<u>Ego</u>—It means the Self in Latin. In this text it refers to the Self, which makes us feel as individuals and observers of the universe around us (individualism). It allows us to perceive what is mine and what belongs to others, and to observe the effects of time (birth, aging, sickness and death) upon us and interpret the quality of life with the feelings generated by our 5 senses, in good and bad experiences. Our personality is born from its experience.

<u>Selfishness</u>—A way to live together in the universe, based on the physical independence and individualism that make us feel artificially separated in races, colors, religions, knowledge and power, where our actions and its effects are not observed as being interdependent. (It's the world of mine and yours, but not of ours!)

<u>Personality</u>—It's the programming (software) that we have been made to believe that defines what we are. It's generated from a combination of the hereditary characteristics from both parents and the acquired or learned experiences of our parents, friends, teachers, religions, books, social environment and communications media.

<u>Transcendent</u>—That which by its nature transcends the physical plane, that some people call the metaphysical. It refers to what is anti-material, where the concepts of time and space do not exist and corresponds to the multidimensional world of antimatter.

<u>Periodic Table</u>—What I call "The Great Symphony of the Chemical Elements". The arrangement of elements in

groups based on each element's atomic number, which classifies them into families with different chemical characteristics.

We must revise the previous chapter and remember that the Self appeared as a manifestation made in the image of Love (God). It manifests in our reality with all the qualities that appeared after the Big Bang in an apparently dual form that we identify as: the qualities of the Son of God (antimatter - Spirit) and those of the Son of Man (matter-time-space), and that dwell and share jointly in the Christ. (The Son of God within the son of man)

What are the qualities of those two natures? Let's see them summarized in the attached table:

(The Self as a Son of Man)	The Self as a Son of Love (God)
Perceivable-Relative Space-Time	Imperceptible-Absolute Without Time-Space
It's deterministic:It's born and dies in the dimension of space and time.	It's probabilistic:Nothing is impossible in this state.Death is a change of manifestation from matter to energy.
It's reductionist:The parts of this universe seem to act independently from others (individualism, selfishness). Every event has an external cause prior to it.	It's holistic: The Universe is a unified holographic whole, whose parts instantaneously interact with each other. Every event in its parts impacts all other parts (Interdependent).

The observer observes the Universe as something outside himself and does not feel a part of it. Reality is external and independent of the observer.	The observer is an interdependent part of his universe. He is a microcosm of his macrocosm, and maintains a holographic relationship with the whole. The universe surrounding him can be changed with his thought intent.
It's based on the knowledge of "absolute truths or laws"Time is absolute everyplace in the universe.The universe is tridimensional.	It's based on the knowledge of a universe that changes continually in infinite cycles with "tendencies to exist" or "tendencies to happen".Time does not exist.The universe is multidimensional.

We must remember that the material universe where we human beings live only occupies 5% of the totality of the universe. It's ruled by the laws of classic physics (check the table in the previous chapter, where time affects its manifestation in the cycles of birth and death and existence is limited to the biological form of life).

From the previous chapter we can understand the paradox created by the apparent duality of a temporal self, who lives in time and in the habits created by his mind, suggesting to him that he has his beginning at birth and his end at death. But does something really die in this universe, or is what happens only an infinite transformation of matter ⟷ energy as Einstein demonstrates in his theory of relativity? (read the topic about the energy transformation law in the glossary). The universe is the most efficient recycling factory that exists, that's why we must be careful that it doesn't recycle us!

It's not reasonable to believe that, since 5% of our self disappears from the material world, we stop existing. It's worth asking, where was the 95 % of my self before birth and where does it go when my body dies? Will we accept that our awareness of self will disappear with our ashes?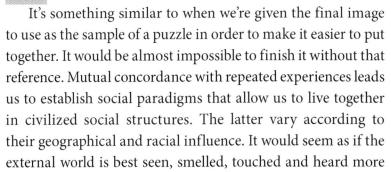

Referring to the poem in this chapter, it's worth asking: why do the rivers (Sons of Man) lose awareness of their origins (ocean-God)? This apparent separation of the Son of Man (time and matter) from its origins, God (antimatter, multidimensional, timeless) begins with the appearance of the concept of Self (ego), when the 5 senses develop in the biological organism.

Scientific studies point us towards highlighting that the process of observing the external universe by means of the 5 senses is a very subjective process entailing interpretation and organization, where we arrange the external world with the help of learning experiences others have previously undergone.

These learned patterns that rule our lives turn into good or bad habits, depending on how they make us feel.

It's something similar to when we're given the final image to use as the sample of a puzzle in order to make it easier to put together. It would be almost impossible to finish it without that reference. Mutual concordance with repeated experiences leads us to establish social paradigms that allow us to live together in civilized social structures. The latter vary according to their geographical and racial influence. It would seem as if the external world is best seen, smelled, touched and heard more with the brain than with the senses per se. We will see further on how quantum physics suggests that the observer influences the manifestation of what is observed. It thus suggests that our experiences about our external reality will vary according to the experiences or habits learned during the process of living them.

Our reality of what we perceive varies according to the color of the lens we use to observe it (learned and inherited patterns / beauty is in the eye of the beholder).

Individualism (Independence) versus Interdependence. The false impression of individualism.

The origin of individualism is based on the apparent onset (physical birth) and the physical dissolution (death) of the temporal manifestation of our immortal origin (God). This transition generates in the individual the concept of time, aging and the sense of urgency to obtain maximum advantage of the period of experience that we call life. Then the human being, based on the fact that he feels he has to take advantage of time to the fullest, decides to search for what satisfies him as a individual and brings him more happiness, without considering the effects these actions may have on others that share his experience. This out of control individualism begets selfishness (ego) and originates Ricky Martin's song, "La Vida Loca" (the thoughtless life). The beings that live in this manner never really find true happiness.

The search for happiness is one of the few actions in which human beings absolutely agree upon, though they may not agree on what it implies or how to find it. This quest for satisfaction emphasizes the creation of physical and mental boundaries that we would like to "privatize" for our welfare and security, trying to keep them unchanged in appearance and actions. That quest is ultimately insatiable and eventually results in more suffering and dissatisfaction.

The result of this search is the unending cycle of change that generates time and the time that generates change (This Zen (Koan) paradox is mine!).

Origins of Suffering

The man who does not understand where he comes from and who he really is, feels lost in an unending battle with the time and change that he himself has created with his habits. He also experiences the discrepancy he has with other beings regarding what happiness really is.

Living, if we go about it with selfishness and lack of awareness about our interdependence with the universal laws and other beings, turns into a nightmare of suffering with brief moments of happiness (it resembles a soap opera).

Happiness is a state of interior balance (wellbeing) of the mind, which does not depend on what's happening outside of itself.

The Son of Man would seem to have forgotten his true origins, by ignorantly creating a fictitious separation from its creator. Then, to find happiness again we must:

Remember our true origins and understand that the experience of life is just one, where the transcendental manifests in an infinite and changing spectrum of possibilities. The interdependence of one possibility with another is inevitable, which gives rise to true solidarity with humanity in this experience. We will then realize that the origin of all of this suffering is ignorance of our true original nature?

All religions emphasized that the human being should understand his transcendental origin in order to find love and peace in his life. (Seems like their followers did not understand the message, no?)

The Bible emphasized the fact that God's Kingdom is not of this world, but paradoxically it could be found in the hearts of all men. (Seems like another Zen Buddhism paradox [Koan]). This is in tune with the dual presence of the nature of the being that we have described. Then we should understand that man was the one that, with his mind, bound himself in his own prison created by the bars of his selfishness (5 senses), and that he later forgot how he existed, outside of it, in the house of His Creator. Are we masochists that only seek to self-flagellate?

The speed of light, the imaginary frontier that divides time from no-time.

Einstein proved that time is relative to the speed of light, where time, for an observer traveling through space, would seem to go slower as the speed of his ship increases. Theoretically, if his speed should reach that of light, time would disappear and his ship would cease existing for other observers in time.

In this way a virtual barrier is created that divides the universe into two parts, one visible in time and the other invisible outside of time for any object that travels at the speed of light.

Since all matter in the universe is composed, in its most essential state, of specific configurations of invisible subatomic particles, which in turn are grouped into visible elements and compounds (periodic table of the elements), we could conclude that our bodies are composed of invisible matter (subatomic particles) and of visible matter (elements and compounds).

If we accept the scientific theory that says that most subatomic particles travel near or at the speed of light, we would have to conclude that they are outside space-time and are invisible to us.

And if we already know that our bodies are made up of 95% subatomic particles that are outside of time (antimatter), there's a part of our bodies that is invisible and out of time and it's immortal! (But, watch what you do, since the mortal part is an unavoidable reality!).

So we are multidimensional travelers, who share the duality of time and timelessness simultaneously, though most of the time we are only aware of our material part within space and time.

Which is the same as to say that we are the Sons of God, living together within the Son of Man!

We could conclude that selfish acts and Man's transgressions of Love originate in his ignorance of his true origin and his true nature as a Son of God ("Forgive them, Father, for they know not what they do").

When men feel like "family", where the blood and genetic inheritance that unites them is the force of Love, the qualities that for so long have been inhibited by ignorance, fear and anger manifest in them spontaneously. Selfishness then vanishes with the sensation of being a part of, and not apart from. As they said in the Three Musketeers, "One for all and all for one!"

This is the way we understand Love as described by St. Paul in his epistle, "Love is patient, love is kind and is not jealous; love does not brag and is not arrogant, does not act unbecomingly; it does not seek its own, is not provoked, does not take into account a wrong suffered, does not rejoice in unrighteousness, but rejoices with the truth; bears all things, believes all things, hopes all things, endures all things. Love never fails".

Homework

Let's review the history of our life. Let's remember its happiest moments. Were those material accomplishments like honors, diplomas, properties, cars or riches? Or were they events that are not so practical, like weddings, the birth of a child or grandchild, a graduation or a loved one's success? How many events stemming from material goals later had consequences that weren't so nice? Like, for example, the responsibility of having to pay of a new car or a home mortgage. These educational goals and diplomas, did they bring what you expected to get from them or did they only add responsibilities and obligations?

All of your planning and goods acquisition and public acknowledgment, could it forestall the many sad moments in your life, like the death and sickness of a loved one or like your parents' divorce within their apparent wealth? How many plastic surgeries will we need to preserve the illusion of eternal youth? There is no surgery that can erase our hearts' emotional scars when they have aged to a point where they can no longer love life's simple things.

Let's review our lives and remember to how many beings we owe all of our accomplishments, and let's be thankful. It's an interminable list, starting with our parents. Now let's meditate silently about all of our experiences and their consequences. Let's realize how our actions affect others, directly and indirectly, and how others' actions have the same effect with us. Do we feel like rivers of the Great Ocean or like rivers that follow their course without reference to their surroundings? Let us finish with a silent meditation. Search again for where your self or mind is.

Bonus questions to improve your grade (10 points/question for bookworms)

1) If happiness is a state of wellness created by the mind, what should I do when facing the experiences of suffering that I undergo, in order to diminish them?
2) Does evil exist in men? If it does not, why do we carry out actions that create suffering in others?
3) Where can we find Love in this world that is so conflictive? (suggestion: look in a mirror!)

What can we do to change learned habits that do not allow us to recognize that we are Sons of God and feel Loved? (suggestion: What do we do with our computers obsolete programs?)

CHAPTER III

OUR UNIVERSE, A TIMELESS STORY

Responsible Co-creation that is born from our free will

Glossary, Chapter III

1) <u>Free Will</u>—Part of the ability of a rational being, whom, within his abilities or limitations, chooses the most beneficial option at a given point in his individual experience. Free will is not the same for everyone: it varies according to individual intelligence, social status, politics, ethics and health. It's associated with a being's will to act with relative freedom. This vision, focused on individualism, generates the extreme individual action known as selfishness.

2) <u>Brain Hemispheres Theory</u>—Neurology and psychology have found that each brain hemisphere predominates for certain tasks. The left hemisphere (reason) processes information analytically and sequentially, step by step, in a logical and linear manner. This hemisphere analyzes, abstracts, counts, measures time, plans procedures step by step, verbalizes and thinks in words and numbers. In other words, it includes the ability for mathematics and for reading and writing. The right hemisphere (Love), on the other hand, seems to be specialized in global perception, synthesizing the information that reaches it. With it we see things in space and how the parts combine

to form the whole. Thanks to the right hemisphere, we understand metaphors, dream, create music and create new idea combinations. It's intuitive and emotional instead of logical. It thinks in images, symbols and feelings. It possesses an imaginative and fantastic ability, spatial and perceptive.

3) <u>Primordial Nature (Love)</u>—What existed before the Big Bang, and the origin of everything. It's the feminine part of the trinity (Yin, or Spirit) and gives birth to the Big Bang (Yang).

4) <u>Co-Creation</u>—It's the process of creation where Love (God) facilitates and empowers his son with free will to create a universe and makes him co-responsible for the results. The final result shall correspond to the loving or selfish intention of the sons of God.

5) <u>Tower of Babel</u>—A tower that the first Hebrew tribes started to build to reach Heaven, since all shared a common language that facilitated the process. God, who did not wish for man to do this, scattered them across the Earth and changed their languages so that they could not understand each other and finish the tower. (How mischievous Yahweh was!)

6) <u>Cosmic Schizophrenia</u>—State of mental confusion where the Self manifests a dual personality, as the son of God or Son of Man, which makes him live in an unbalanced universe and causes him a lot of confusion and suffering. Most of these think themselves to be only sons of man and consider that those who believe that they are sons of God are crazy.

7) <u>Shamata</u>—Meditation technique whose purpose is to soothe the mind, focusing it on an object or action. (Ex. candles, statues, actions, music, prayers, mantras or repetitive acts).

In this chapter, we will focus on trying to clarify a bit more the question: Who am I?

Our understanding of the universe is like a story without a beginning or end where the reader is creating the plot as he is reading the story

Summing up the first two chapters, we could conclude that we live in a universe with an apparent dual manifestation, created by the contrasts originated by the Self's dual nature as it is perceived by means of the 5 senses. In these two chapters we discussed the duality of a perceivable world that represents a 5% and an imperceptible one that represents the 95%, respectively, of the existing universe. With the inconvenience that man lives mainly aware of the 5% that he perceives, generating conflictive barriers between his two natures that do not allow him to really understand himself like the Greek philosophers and the teachings of the Far East suggested.

Man would seem to be living in a *cosmic schizophrenia*, where the humans accompanying him on the path consider that he is normal because they share his same hallucinations, ¡but consider stark raving mad those who speak to them about the imperceptible world of Love! (Hence the phrase "Falling madly in Love").

The duality of human beings

Throughout history, this dual nature of man was the theological basis of nearly all existing religions and philosophies. For purposes of our discussion, we could classify it as:

- ◆ Absolute-imperceptible nature (transcendental, immaterial, transparent, immutable and immeasurable)
- ◆ Relative-perceivable nature (apparent, material, dense, changing and perishable) (see the table in the previous chapter)

This whole situation generates some existential questions. Are we material beings limited by the laws of time and matter? Are we spiritual beings with a material manifestation that is independent of its origin? Are we beings with the two natures manifesting simultaneously, where one or the other predominates from moment to moment, depending on many factors? What I have learned from my many blunders in the School Of Life after repeating several classes, suggests to me that the affirmative reply to the last question is the most appropriate one. The problem lies in that man is mainly aware of the relative one and it's hard for him to comprehend the absolute one. These two natures are present in human beings in a continually varying interaction that allows for the predominance of one or the other due to the influence of the following factors:

- ◆ The person's ability for realizing the existence of these natures (this is the most important step in order to be able to pass the final exam in the School of Life)

- The ability to understand his origins
- The ability to understand how they interact
- The ability to understand how these influence his life perspective (happiness or suffering)
- The communications breakdown between the two natures, humanity's Tower of Babel, and the origin of our Cosmic Schizophrenia

These abilities depend on the efficient intercommunication between the two natures.

The main problem is that the languages used by these to try to communicate with each other are incompatible. Relative nature, like the left side of the brain, uses reason and scientific laws, while the absolute, like the right half, uses intuition and Love as the basis for communication.

This lack of synchronization between our brain hemispheres is the source of our cosmic schizophrenia. Relative nature is deterministic and organized. The absolute one is spontaneous and probabilistic. This separation generated by the language divergence between the two natures (brain hemispheres) would somewhat resemble what happened during the construction of the Tower of Babel in the Old Testament, which spawned all of humanity's diverging races and customs.

The only possible way to reestablish communications between both is to find a common language. This is facilitated by prayer and meditation, which have been the traditional methods encouraged by all religious philosophies. The only thing that has the ability to coordinate this new link is the language of Love that resides in our heart (right brain hemisphere).

The difficulty in accomplishing this action lies in getting the self's rational side (left brain hemisphere or reason) to sit at the negotiating table to speak with the spiritual side (right brain hemisphere or heart).

The problem is that the self's rational side, which is mostly guided by the laws of reason and science (which only apply to 5% of his existential reality), is afraid of losing the hegemony which it has maintained for such a long time. This existential conflict between the two natures has been the origin of humanity's suffering throughout history.

Man, like the prodigal son, separates from his true origins and home (spiritual kingdom) by voluntarily requesting his material inheritance (free will, reason, temporal life), then lives as oriented by his material side in a life of selfishness and individual satisfaction. That initially pleasant experience gradually degenerates into a progressive dissatisfaction and unhappiness that time, aging and existential loneliness generate in the self until, later, he finally understands that he had always enjoyed true happiness at his father's house (the kingdom of the spirit and love).

It's then that, in his saddest moments, the Son of Man finally acknowledged his true origin and listens to his transcendent side (Heart) and decides to return to his true home. To his surprise, the symbol of Love represented by his Father's forgiveness happily welcomes him and celebrates his return, since he had left home as the Son of Man, yet comes back transformed as the Son of God, the Christ or the Buddha that potentially resides in every one of us!

We're then left to ponder, what would have happened if the prodigal son had not experienced, while using his free will, the experience of creation? Wouldn't it have been easier for the

Father, in His wisdom, to forestall his son from the experience of suffering by nagging him about what was going to happen, even knowing that the son would not pay attention to it? Isn't that what most fathers-mothers would have done?

From this experience of apparent suffering arises the empathy and compassion that turns the Son of Man into Son of God.

Wouldn't this be the only way for the son of man to spread the true inheritance of his Father (Love) throughout the universe, where he would be like the image of Love in the mirror of creation, where his fellow man would see himself reflected in it? (This phrase is like a supersized combo of your favorite *fast food*. Watch it so you don't get mental indigestion!)

Co-Creation. A Compassionate and Responsible Vision of the Universe

Where does the perceivable (tangible) essence of our universe originate? (check the first chapter) Does it develop independently of our ability to perceive by means of predetermined laws or forces, or is it influenced by the subjective individual viewpoint of human beings? This question has promoted the development of endless explanations outlined by many philosophical schools. I will try to present a synthesis of what I have obtained through my contact with various philosophies.

The prevailing position based on proven scientific laws tends to posit that everything that exists occurs independently of human beings' perception, insofar as matter and energy interrelate, and emphasizing the fact that only that which can be verified via the scientific method exists.

The problem with this position is that new discoveries continually render inoperable many scientific laws of the past, creating never-ending changes in our concept of the prior material world. Thus, yesterday's scientific law may turns into tomorrow's lie.

The science of the new quantum physics, of the theory of relativity, the theory of multiple dimensions and theoretical analytical mathematics, questions this deterministic scientific viewpoint. It suggests to us that time is a relative phenomenon and that what happens in the material word is intimately affected by the observer. It also tells us that we can theorize the presence of multiple invisible dimensions besides the three that rule our visible universe.

But, how is it that the universe's most elemental components group together into ever more complex organizations, until they manifest in the visible material world?

Why does science, as it studies the microcosm (the world of the tiny and invisible) and the macrocosm (the visible world) finds that it does not seem to have a beginning nor an end, and that the scientific laws that rule its order seem to constantly change?

An example of this in the microcosm are the endless types and amounts of subatomic particles that have been discovered since the atom's basic structure was initially discovered and described as limited to protons, neutrons and electrons.

A possible theory is the one suggested by quantum physics, whereby the observer's (subject) subjective influence over the elemental components of the invisible universe (object) affects the way in which they behave and manifest in the universe. According to this theory, the universe's primordial matter (antimatter?) exists in a potential state where all of the endless possibilities of its possible manifestation exist and which depends on how the observer organizes them.

Our understanding of the universe is like a tale without beginning or end, where the reader creates the script as he reads along. It's like the act of creation was more like an act of facilitation, where Love (divinity) is the facilitator and mankind's mind, with its free will, is the co-creator.

The important thing in this sort of book is that depending on the reader's free will and viewpoint regarding his nature, the script will be full of happiness or suffering. This is determined by the prevalence of the person's viewpoint (selfishness) of the left brain hemisphere or the interdependent (loving, supportive) of the right brain hemisphere. We could also say that it depends on the preponderance of Reason (brain) versus Love (heart, intuition). There's plenty of ground to cover here!

The universe we know might then be visualized as a collection of habits or concordant viewpoints that, based on the probability that they might occur within a particular time frame, and with the coinciding observation by a group of persons, turn into paradigms acceptable to said groups.

The more repeatedly these paradigms agree in an observation, the latter becomes more real or true for observers.

It's as if we were organizing the endless potential of the primordial matrix (Love), as per our subjective viewpoint and we later become attached to it as if it constituted an absolute truth, which we will later transmit to others until we convince them too. We act like madmen guiding other madmen or the blind leading the blind! (fanaticism and prejudices).

When scientific methods are used and the subjectivity of observed occurrences is controlled, science terms them scientific laws.

These laws are like snapshots that freeze the continuous creativity of the primordial nature of the universe, Love, in time. Afterwards, the mind reconstructs them in a fictitious continuity, like a movie edited from 3 hours down to 1, created by the mind's subjective changing nature. Resulting in that most of the original important experiences and essence of the movie are lost in that edited cut.

The same thing happens in the development of the laws that regulate the sociocultural style of different countries and races, based on their group and individual experiences. Just observe the differences between what different races consider delicious foods and you will see what I mean.

If we return to the original questions, we would have to agree that we are beings manifesting both natures simultaneously, where one or the other predominates from moment to moment, depending on many factors.

It seems to me that, after the previous discussion, we could conclude that time is relative, that the perceivable minority manifestation (5%) is created artificially by the mind of the observer, and that its dissolution (death) in the relative time of the visible universe does not affect the creative potential of the imperceptible nature (95%). We also see that the infinite matrix (transcendence, Divinity, Love) and its temporal manifestation (the material universe) are involved in an intimate interrelationship of a continually shifting nature. (Don't worry be happy, life is but a dream!)

In other words, the observer could turn the universe into whatever he desired just by establishing an open and unimpeded communication with his primordial nature, guided in his free will by Love. Could this be an act of what is called Faith?

If that is so, we must learn to reduce the predominance of the relative and perishable part of our self, to allow the absolute or transcendental one to participate within the mind's creative process and thus modify the individualism and separatism created by selfishness. In this way, you promote the solidarity born of the interdependence of feeling that we are a Universal Family, as true Sons of God.

This would be the purest way to manifest Love in the universe in an act of Loving co-creation and co-responsibility!

The relativistic mind (that 5%), which is the creator of the duality that separates us from our true nature, is always engaging in frenetic activity to maintain the apparent reality of our material universe stable, with all of its laws and consequences.

Thus life may turn into an endless display of contrasts the mind of the son of man classifies, as per its individual perception and experience, into good, bad or neutral. And then promotes actions that attract the good, repel the bad and creates indifference for the neutral ones.

This generates an interminable cycle of pleasing experiences when we obtain the good contrasts and of disagreeable ones when we don't. As the relative presence of time generates an inevitable change in the universe, it's impossible for man to avoid the cycles of good experiences along with the bad ones. There's no perfect climate, there's no delicacy that will not rot, there's no harvest to be had without work, there's no metal that will not corrode, there's no permanent personal relationship or a body that will not age and die.

Let's all then learn to make our tale one of Love and solidarity, with a happy ending for all characters!

Bonus questions to improve your grade (10 points/question for bookworms)

1) How does the intent of our free will influence our role in the book or theater of life? How can we improve our prominence in the play?
2) Is free will really free?
3) Seek examples of cases of Cosmic Schizophrenia in your own lives and those of others.
4) Let's imagine examples of how to use co-creation and co-responsibility in our lives at home, at work and in politics.
5) Examine your previous concept of Faith and study the one mentioned in this chapter. Why can't Faith guarantee that your desires become true when you wish them to be? (suggestion: study the difference between relative time of the Son of Man and absolute time of the Son of God)
6) How can we increase the possibilities that something that I want will happen? Suggestion: study the intention and the sum of all beliefs of the Sons of Man in our vision of the universe.

Reflection and Meditation Exercise

To decrease the predominance of the self's relative (rational) part, we must learn to pacify it. The technique for pacifying the mind is the object of the meditation termed Shamata, where we focus the mind's action in a single direction. Though techniques vary a lot, the most used ones focus on sacred objects, a light like a candle's, saying the Rosary, or singing a mantra. In the Tibetan Buddhist tradition, focusing thought on the breathing cycle is encouraged, observing how air enters and exits the nose while we allow the cycle to proceed in a natural way. Practice counting breathing cycles that consist of one inhalation and one exhalation, up to seven times. The moment the mind detours thought towards something else, you must restart counting the 7 breaths cycle. You will be surprised how fast the mind detours before the seventh cycle! Again, seek where the self or the mind is located in your bodies.

CHAPTER IV

"GOD'S NAME IS SO LARGE IT WON'T FIT IN MY MOUTH."

**Experiences that separate us. The origin
of religious discrepancies.**

Glossary, Chapter IV

1) <u>Rosetta Stone</u> – A stone found during excavations of the ancient Egyptian civilization, which yielded the key for translating hieroglyphs.

In order to understand from where our discrepancies come from, we must first review the factors that influence the way in which our dual natures present and produce an expression of our awareness or a way of seeing this universe.

The preponderance of one or another manifestation of these dual natures in the conscience of an affected person depends on several factors:

1) The person's ability to realize the dual natures' existence. We must understand that they exist due to scientific evidence, even though we may not perceive all of them.
2) The ability to understand their origin. (Review Chapter I)
3) The ability to understand how they interact.

4) The ability to understand how they influence your vision of life (happiness or suffering).

Realizing these abilities depends on efficient inter-communication between the two natures that we symbolically represent as right hemisphere (spirit-intuition-timeless) and left hemisphere (matter–time-reason).

The first two can be understood within the context of our temporal universe, since it is through reason and science that we can infer their answers. If you examine what's written in the previous chapters we could conclude that:

1) Our universe and our bodies are composed of two forms of existence.
2) One, ruled by the laws of time and scientific knowledge, is perceivable and demonstrable by our 5 senses and has an apparent beginning (birth) and end (death). We scientifically know that these make up 5% of the potential universe.
3) The other, inferred from quantum physics and from the discoveries of the theory of general relativity, tells us that the remaining 95% of the universe is invisible to our 5 senses, and that the invisible universe's elemental component is what gives rise to the visible one. We must then realize that the last one will be outside the rules of time-space, because it has no beginning or end.

We could thus accept that we, as well as the universe, are made out of a tapestry woven of two types of thread or filaments (antimatter and matter), but that our senses can only be aware of one of these threads (matter).

Perhaps the threads of the tunic in the fairy tale, "The Emperor's new clothes", was made with antimatter!

Assuming that my previous discussion has convinced you of the existence of both natures, how can we then find a way to reestablish communication between both and what will the consequences of this reunification? Let's remember that the languages of each of these are not compatible, and that we have to find the Rosetta Stone that gives us the key to remember our universal language, lost since the Tower of Babel, and thus be able to communicate with our imperceptible nature. Let's leave the discussion of this communication enigma aside for later, and let's get into the communication problems that exist in the visible universe of the 5 senses.

Communication Problems in the Realm of Matter-Time. The battle between the two brain hemispheres: Right-Intuition, Left-Reason. (Remember the cartoons with the little white and black angels fighting for the attention of the character?)

The same as there exist virtual barriers between the material and the immaterial universe, there are similar barriers between the mini-universes created by individualism in the mind of humans.

These barriers, limitations created by the 5 senses perceiving individual experiences and abilities, are the interferences that sow discord and unhappiness among human beings and between the two brain hemispheres.

This leads to divergent views of reality that are influenced by race, socioeconomic status, geographical location and religion.

It's logical and obvious that sociocultural customs and laws that govern different nations are subjectively influenced by the preceding. One of the most outstanding are the differences between women's human rights in diverse societies and religions. We know that dissimilar experiences in upbringing, education and religion that happen even among different economic and racial backgrounds in the same country produce significant lifestyle discrepancies.

 "The name of God is so large it will not fit in my mouth." (modified quote from the Hebrew Cabbalistic tradition).

These communication problems among men amplify their communications problem with their transcendental origin, creating infinite discrepancies in humanity's religious views. Since I was a young man I was always intrigued by problems created by divergent religious visions as to God's nature (the transcendent nature), that has even been the main reason for most of history's armed conflicts.

Allow me to tell you how my interpretation of that experience helped me to find the way out of this quagmire. Let's assume for the moment that most of us agree in that there's only one transcendent reality. Let's make a comparison that will allow us to understand where so many divergences arise from, even though it's somewhat simplistic in its approach:

Let's compare the transcendent Nature (God) (Love) to a great, universal radio broadcasting station with certain features:

1) It transmits 24 hours a day, 7 days a week since beginningless time.

2) Its broadcasting range is infinite since it has no limits in space or time.

3) It transmits its message without interference, since it does it from the other side of the interferences, where there is no duality of manifestations from material laws.

4) The essence of the message is the same: the purest manifestation of Love. It manifests with infinite qualities, perceivable in the earthly world and bringing happiness to every being according to their needs, (Compassion, Wisdom, Tolerance, Understanding, Flexibility, Empathy, Patience, etc.).

5) The broadcast has the flexibility to adapt to the listening capacity of the receiving radio.

Interferences of the Receiving Radio – The Source of the Problem

Though human beings are made in the image and likeness of Transcendent Nature, they are limited by interference inherent to their material nature (5 senses and their individual experience). These limitations of the receiving radio are the source of all apparent divergence in the view of the material universe. Limited to time and the perceivable world, the receiving radio has some limitations when relaying the signal to others, mainly these are:

- It does not rebroadcast all the time.
- Its free will allows it to turn its radio on, tune in to the right or wrong station or to keep it off.
- Many of us don't turn the radio on, because mainly, we are not aware of the radio, and live alienated in our material world. Others, though we turn the radio on,

only seek stations that reinforce our individualism. We like what reinforces living la Vida Loca!

- ♦ The purity of the reception is determined by the limitations of the material world (by the interference from the 5 senses, intellectual capacity, socioeconomic situation, education and religious concepts).

This promotes the creation of a tunnel vision of the original message by each being's individuality (ego), (we resemble horses with blinders on, guided by the jockey of our 5 senses).

"The name of God is so large it will not fit in my mouth."

This phrase, which I adapted from the Hebrew Scriptures, comes from the respect they had for the sacred name of God. From the Cabalistic Hebrew teachings, according to their interpretation of the Old Testament, it was explained to me that there were many names to describe God, since the qualities of his influence were so varied. However, there was only one written form or sacred syllables that gave rise to all the other names, which form was unpronounceable and a sacrilege to pronounce.

When I heard this, I immediately rebuked the teacher: "How, then, will I be able to refer to that manifestation of God, breaking the Hebrew tradition?" He replied: You only have to refer to Him as "He whose name is so immeasurably enormous that it will not fit in my mouth." My interpretation of that phrase takes a less literal turn since it reflects the complexity and infinity of the concept of divinity for the individual in the world of the 5 senses.

As the perceiver is ruled by time and his senses, it's impossible for him to perceive the totality of the immensity of the transcendent without first reducing (interpreting) it to an understandable size (chewable and digestible). This view, though very real in his individual experience, is very influenced by his life experience.

Human beings, in their search for transcendence, when they sense a signal from the Great Radio Broadcaster do not realize that they perceive a very limited and individual part of the transmission (tunnel vision). Though this vision may inspire them and fill them with happiness and hope, this is only a part of the divinity's immensity and does not necessarily have to mesh with that of other individuals who are also in tune with the great universal radio transmitter.

The mistake many men make is that, instead of thinking that man is made in the image and likeness of the divinity, erroneously think that God is made in the image and likeness of man. We all know people who believe this, isn't it true?

The Incomplete Rebroadcast and the Amplification of the Original Interpretative Mistake in Communication

The Self, in its happiness of wanting to share this message with others, begins to rebroadcast it with its interferences (limitations of the 5 senses) and those of the receivers. The message is distorted when shared with others, the same as what happens when a group whispers a message, which when it reaches the last person in the chain is unrecognizable.

Many others who have also contacted the original message and seen it their way (as Frank Sinatra said) will find various discrepancies with their view, thus begetting the first religious divergences.

Men, seeking their origins, do not realize that they are all receiving a very personal and true message for each one. Yet, they forget that others are also receiving it according to their own nature. Perhaps the easiest way to get to know God would be by learning from all of the individual views of every man, since "the Kingdom of God is in the heart of all men".

We could then postulate that, in order to improve relations and the life experience that we share, we would have to improve communications at all levels simultaneously and between all components that take part in it.

- Man's communication with the transcendent (God).
- Man with himself.
- Man with others.

The quality and purity of the communication that will happen among the previous two levels will be directly proportional to the communication man establishes with the transcendent nature.

This implies that the most adequate way to know oneself is by knowing the divinity and seeing how it manifests itself in its individual universe (Self). Then, acknowledging that this divinity is also shared with all other men and that it leads them to acknowledge humanity's true bond of solidarity, created by the shared lineage of Love. The phrase "Love thy neighbor like thyself" is born of this relationship that automatically generates the Golden Rule: "Do not do to others what you would not want done to you" and the resulting" "Do to others what you would want done to you."

This interaction between the two natures is continuously going on, since the great station is continually broadcasting, but its influence depends on man's free will to tune in or not, and on which station he prefers. (Do you understand now how we self-flagellate with the whip of selfishness?)

We can't then blame or place responsibility on others or on the divinity's intervention for the suffering we have created with our selfish actions, due to our, or other people's ignorance (Forgive them, for they know not what they do!).

The divinity's Love is like that of a Universal Mother (Love) that considers all sons of creation as beings that she loves the same, and whom she allows to learn from their experience at their own pace, without preconceived expectations. The self fools himself when he believes he is a favorite of the great Universal Mother. As the song in Spanish goes,

"Divine illusion...
That I built
It was a dream...
that didn't come true"

But how can we learn to see the universe with the eyes of the spirit? The capacity to balance our two abilities will provide the mechanism. The next chapter's topic will be an explanation of how to carry out the following.

- The ability to understand how they interact.
- The ability to understand how these influence our view of life (Happiness or suffering). (This is the chapter that will resemble a tragic Mexican soap opera!)

Bonus questions to improve your grade (10 points/ question for bookworms)

1) Is there a religion that conveys God's (Love's) nature in its totality?
2) Why is history full of religion-based armed conflicts?
3) How can the Self improve its communication with other Selves?
4) How can it improve its communication with God?
5) Let's seek the basis for forgiveness by reviewing the previous chapters. What is the main basis for each of the Self's selfish actions?

Reflection and Meditation Exercise

Besides repeating the one from the previous chapter, let's dedicate our day to carefully observing our interaction with our environment. Let's observe our daily routines, like our personal hygiene, dressing (which shoe you put on first? Which sleeve do you put your arm down first?) Note your breakfast routine. Observe your breathing cycle, and note the difference in rhythm and temperature between breathing in and breathing out. All along your ritual, observe what you mind is doing. Try to chew your food at least twenty times and be aware of the flavors. Avoid controversial topics and discussions during your meals. Is your mind wandering elsewhere or in other actions? Practice taking it to the present action. Observe well your interaction with colleagues at work and try to pinpoint how they feel: are they happy or sad? Note how you feel emotionally regarding each one of them. Why do you like some of them (sympathize) more than others? What factors led you to this conclusion?

The next time that you feel bothered by a colleague's action or comment, ask yourself if his or her intention was to bother you or if you have misinterpreted the action. If we undergo a disagreeable experience of this sort, after calming down, let him or her know that you felt hurt by that action without blaming or criticizing. And observe his or her reaction. When you leave home, smile even at your shadow and observe the effect it has on others. Please don't do this only with the opposite sex, even though you may be single! Before losing emotional control, count until you tire or add complex numbers in your mind! This activates the rational part of your brain and will help you avoid a lot of bother. Reread all previous chapters and learn to see the universe with the eyes of the Spirit.

CHAPTER V

"WHEN THE SELF LEARNS TO SEE THE UNIVERSE THROUGH THE EYES OF THE SPIRIT (HEART), HE ONLY SEES LOVE."

The encounter of our natures at the negotiating table (the Heart).

Glossary, Chapter V

1) <u>Interdependence</u> – The natural state of the universe, which reflects its holographic nature and where all of its parts are woven together by the strings of Love. In this state, an action or effect on one of its parts reverberates across the whole universe. It represents the unity and solidarity of the entire creation (like in the Three Musketeers, "One for all and all for one").

In the previous chapter, after establishing the existence of our two natures, we discussed the way in which we can reestablish communications between them (meditation)

In this chapter we will focus on trying to understand how they interact, how they influence one another, how they manifest in the universe and how they influence our way of looking at life with happiness or suffering.

How can we sit these 2 natures at the negotiating table (heart) and get them to accept one way of interacting that will lead to the individual's happiness as well as that of the totality of the universe, thus achieving a harmony of interdependence between both?

We have already discussed how the material-time part, guided by the limitations of the five senses, created a state of individualism or selfishness where each being that lives within time feels independent from other beings and from its environment. We describe that state as a prison created by the mind of man, where the bars are made out of the metal of time and space (the 5 senses - My right brain in poetic action!).

And we discussed how time creates the illusion of birth and death, prioritizing the aspect of the self's material nature, thus generating the anxiety of trying to take advantage of existence in and efficient and pleasant manner in the briefest time possible. We also mentioned that all beings agree in the search for individual happiness but that, due to their different individual views, disagree as to how to obtain that happiness. That is why opposite poles attract.

The problem created by this view springs from men's apparent individualism and independence, which promote their also-apparent free will. This generates actions that create happiness in some but suffering for others. History is full of examples of how this has happened since the beginning of life on this planet and that are still happening with the exploitation of man and nature by man.

Reestablishing our communication, seated at the negotiating table.

In the beginning we mentioned that the problem was the language discrepancy between the 2 natures, created by the time barrier, and that we would have to find a key that would join the languages or a passageway or gap that would allow us to join both worlds.

Let's remember that initially it was the thought process occurring in the mind of man that created the time barrier when it divided the two worlds. Then the key to harmonizing the apparent discrepancy might lie in reevaluating the thought process with the new data.

From the beginning of the search for the origins of man and the establishment of the different religious concepts of the creative divinity, communications pathways were usually established through third parties (messengers) or by supernatural processes. However, the most common way to establish communication was always prayer and meditation.

The problem with prayer is that, due to limitations inherent in its own nature, man establishes it in only one direction, mostly towards the divinity, thus creating an inevitable interference in communication. By definition, in any kind of communication, a process is begun whereby a message is sent and then the initiator stops his activity to see if he receives a reply.

There cannot be real communication between two parties if we don't receive confirmation or a reaction to our remittance, thus establishing a bidirectional communication!

If the preceding statement is true, the only solution to the enigma of our cosmic schizophrenia is, first, to accept the presence of our transcendental origin. Then, we have to reestablish communications (the connection) with it and sit at the negotiating table (heart).

When the Self finally breaks the illusory barrier of individualism, and looks through the eyes of the spirit, then it has a broader view of the universe. It's as one who looks at his valley after climbing his region's highest mountain. "When then self looks at the Universe, through the eyes of the spirit it only finds Love." This phrase emphasizes the maternal aspect of the universal force of Love, cited in St. Paul's epistle,

> *"Love is patient; love is kind; love is not envious or boastful or arrogant or rude. It does not insist on its own way; it is not irritable or resentful; it does not rejoice in wrongdoing, but rejoices in the truth. It bears all things, believes all things, hopes all things, endures all things. Love never ends."*

Man's true free will is born from this force of Love, this journey in the world of time and matter (space), which makes him co-responsible for his actions and their consequences during his visit. As in the world of matter and energy, according to Newton's laws, every action has a similar and proportional reaction to the original one in order to preserve balance in the universe.

That's why every action that happens in the Universe is interdependent (has repercussions on all parties), including those executed by man. And from these observations we see the logic in the Golden Rule, again: "Do not do unto others what you would not want done to yourself."

We also established that man, in his material nature, has limitations that do not allow a clear understanding of his universe due to interferences created by the limitations of the 5 sense and by his individual experience as per his upbringing, education, social level, religious views and race.

It was discussed that those men whom, when experiencing some form of intercommunication with their transcendent nature (the Great Universal Radio Broadcaster), have individual interferences that allow him to perceive a valid but very limited view of transcendent reality that can create discrepancies in the conception of the divinity.

This realization should unite us and help us to listen, learn and have tolerance for the infinite ways in which men perceive God's nature.

Most religious prayers are of the unidirectional kind we previously mentioned, like the "sound heard when a tree falls in a lonely forest". If we don't hear anything at the end of the prayer, it will seem to fall on deaf ears.

The meditation's purpose as the prayer's final part is to establish receptivity and tune in to the best station with less interference. Depending on the religious philosophy, there are several meditation techniques, but all coincide in trying to quiet thought activity and establish a mental state of maximum relaxation and harmony. Modern research has shown that this mental state harmonizes brain waves, besides many other beneficial aspects of human physiology.

Therefore, the key to exiting the prison created by our minds is the quieting of mental activity through meditation. Meditation is the Rosetta Stone that allows us to intercommunicate openly our two natures (brain hemispheres) under a universal language: Love.

Visualize that the virtual barrier that divides our two natures is created by the mind's (Ego's) continual babbling, in its incessant effort to preserve the sand castles that the waves of the sea of time repeatedly destroys.

To find the gaps in this wall we have to decrease the activity of the energy that creates it, which is thought, until it ceases for a few instants, allowing us to find passageways that give us a glimpse of what lies on the other side. The great Masters of all religious philosophies were able to destroy the barrier in their meditative states, achieving a harmonious union between both worlds.

These great beings learned to see the universe and men with the eyes of the spirit, showering Love upon all of creation.

At the end of this chapter we could conclude that the interaction between our two natures is such that the transcendent, which exists outside of time, begets the material that lives influenced by time. But the self and its individuality (ego) in most cases is not aware of its true origins, initiating an apparent disconnect between both natures (cosmic schizophrenia). This disconnection plus the influence of time and its laws, results in the fictitious appearance of individualism and selfishness. This finally leads to the ongoing contrasts of happiness and suffering in its life (the prison created by its 5 senses).

After the self recognizes its origins and sits at the negotiating table (heart), and wields the key of meditation to free itself from the jail that it created with its own mind, it finds itself gazing at itself with the eyes of the Spirit and finds only Love in creation. And as I said in my poem at the beginning, "This new vision that is born out of our own heart and out of all the beings in this universe, sweeps away from our self every vestige of suffering when we comprehend that Happiness has always accompanied us in this path without beginning or end."

Bonus questions to improve your grade (10 points/ question for bookworms)

1) Seek examples in your life of the different types of interferences that interrupt communication between our two natures.
2) Explain the differences in kinds of communications between prayer and meditation.
3) Explain how cosmic schizophrenia can lead you to depression, anxiety and anger. Identify the triggering factors in your life that provoke its manifestation.
4) Delve deeper into the concept of life as a prison created by our own mind. Study your preferences, habits and customs and see which help you to live and harmony and peace with yourself and with other beings and which are obstacles to living in solidarity.
5) Why does always assuming that we can be wrong in every interpretation of our exchanges with others could help us live more happily?

Exercise in meditation and reflection

After reviewing our previous practices, today we'll use our imagination and visualization. These are other ways to focus the mind similar to breathing, but these have subliminal effects upon our mental state. Depending on your personal beliefs about the divinity, you may use religious figures or symbols that pertain to the former. For example, a Christian may use Christian figures, a practitioner of Oriental philosophies will use his own and someone who sees the divinity in a more impersonal way will do it with symbols of light, color, etc. After calming the mind the breathing exercises, let's project the figure in our minds in full color and tridimensional, a little higher than our sight line, and let's visualize it streaming infinite rays of multicolored light which reach our heart as blessings in all the qualities of Love. Feel the sensation that these soothe our emotional upheavals such as anger, hate, sadness, resentments, guilt, etc.

 ## A colorful bath of Love

Seated in a comfortable position with our back straight head held up high, lets visualize a source of spiritual strength or energy that makes us feel protected. For example, the figure of the Sacred Heart of Jesus, young-looking, smiling and standing, with open arms and beaming rays of multicolored light from the center of His heart to ours, in which a small seed exists.

Let's understand the meaning of the exercise. Jesus represents the human manifestation of the Holy Spirit which is the force of Love that God left us after his Son left. The multicolored rays represent the infinite ways in which Love can manifest among us. The seed in our heart represents the latent form in which Love dwells in man.

As those rays of light fill our heart, let us feel ourselves loved and protected by the Love of God and let's observe how the small seed starts to open and in turn beams the multiple colors of Love in all directions. Initially, let's imagine that those colors bathe us in love and penetrate every part of our bodies, especially those where there is a discomfort, and let's see how the latter is soothed and healed.

After we have been filled with happiness and wellness, we're going to share this with all human beings, especially with those who have hurt us due to their ignorance of love.

Let's visualize that multicolored rays beam from our heart towards all human beings without distinction, including those who have left this world, and those that, in our thoughts, have brought suffering to our lives. Let's dedicate some minutes to this action and then let's rest our mind in silence for a few more minutes. Let's finish by giving thanks for this opportunity. Let's do this exercise ever day upon waking and when going to sleep.

Finally, to keep our mind in a peaceful state, let's imagine that our thoughts are as clouds in the sky and that our natural peaceful state is like the blue color in the sky. Let our thoughts pass like clouds, without following them, focusing on the blueness of the sky, our natural state.

The Melodious Silence Of The Cosmos

Silence yearns to quench the Soul's
unending thirst for Love, yet in its
splendor, it fails to muffle the continuous
yet fleeting chatter of the ego;
for the Soul has long forgotten its majestic tranquility.

How will I be able, then, to arouse again the remembrance
of its melodious song?
I have already realized that this will not
occur by increasing the volume
of the dissonant notes of my mundane life.
Nor by recalling all the memories of my
frivolous experiences, which only
ignite more the flames of my insatiable desire for them.

Nor by reigniting the infernal passions
that muted even more my
sense of hearing.

How can I stifle then the deafening shame of the
condemning voices that punish my heart?
Perhaps only by realizing that all my
lapses were committed with
innocence of intention, and stipulated by
the ignorance of my divine linage.
Clearly established by our great Teacher, Jesus,
who in his last words said, "Father, forgive them,
for they do not know what they are doing."

My heart then finally finds peace, as I understand that
in the forgiveness of my transgressions, and those done to
me by others, resides the final solution to my paradox.
And then, suddenly, a thunderous emptiness permeates
every corner of my Universe, reawakening in my
heart the Melodious Silence of the Cosmos.

CHAPTER VI

THE PARALLEL WORLDS CREATED BY OUR MIND.

"The Blind in Spirit Never Find Love".

When we apply the Golden Rule to intercommunication between men, we allow Love to guide our minds.

We already mentioned in other chapters how each person's individual experience, according to his genetic and sociocultural baggage and the habits or customs that arise from the former, creates infinite ways to see our world. We also spoke about how these perceptions generate agreements or discrepancies in the life that we establish to govern our lives in harmony or discord. We must also remember that "The search for happiness is one of the few actions in which human beings agree absolutely, though we may not agree in what it is and how to find it." Ironically, a substantial part of humanity's suffering arises from this discrepancy in the search for happiness.

We could say that from the infinite, individual and divergent ways of looking at life, man creates parallel mental worlds. These mental worlds isolate him progressively in his already existing vacuum or existential loneliness. That is why I mention in my poem that loneliness "...still exists among the multitude and the bustle." And in another chapter, "And this existential loneliness is nothing less than the jail that he creates in this mind, with the bars of time."

The gathering of individuals in groups and of groups in more complex social organizations led to the development of societies that have nurtured our history. Without delving into the complexity of the individual's relationship within the socioeconomic and political systems that have governed the history of man, I'd like to limit this discussion to the individual's immediate interrelationship with the other persons that are a part of his social milieu, like for example his role in the family, work and religious activities.

We already mentioned in preceding chapters that a good communication between the beings in this universe depends on how good was the communication that man had with his transcendent nature (God), and that all intercommunication levels are limited by the individual experience that man obtains while observing the universe with his 5 senses. In relation to communications in our daily lives, man does not realize that there's a paradox between what he thinks, what he says and what he wants to say, since they don't always coincide. Another discrepancy is that which exists between what he hears, what another person said, and his interpretation of what he heard.

(Proverbs 10:19 put it more elegantly when it said, "*When words are many, sin is not absent, but he who holds his tongue is wise*").

If this is a proven fact, what can we be sure about in our interpretation of what we observe? We also have to take into account that, of the messages in our nonverbal communication, which science tells us that only 7 % of comprehension is based on the words that we use, 13 % are based on the voice, the expression, intonation, etc., and 80% in body language. That's why I humorously say that, in order to stop the incessant jabbering of a Latino, we only have to tie his hands!

What can we do to improve our communication? The final goal is to eliminate all interferences. Later in the book we will highlight the meditation techniques to decrease interferences.

The first thing is to establish a bidirectional conversation with our transcendent reality (God, spirit etc.) which implies using:

1) Prayer—Talking—from us to It. (God)
2) Meditation—Hearing—from them and God to us (there are persons that never have time or are too occupied to listen)

This connection with the divinity slowly changes the way we look at the world through the eyes of the spirit, eliminating all interferences that selfishness has created with the 5 senses.

Let's see some frequent obstacles to our good inter-communication in daily life.

Difficult people in our life (the unloved ones, those who don't know what they're doing) or The Blind of Spirit

Though difficult people come in endless varieties, all have a common basis: they have very poor self-esteem, with scant tolerance for criticism and limited introspection of how their actions affect others.

They, the selfish ones, are like spiritual lame people who use other beings as crutches to walk on the path of life. And they are the Blind of Spirit who never find Love, because they do not know how to love and do not let themselves be loved.

These are the ones who were not loved during their upbringing and never learned to love! I'll call thm "the unloved ones". You can hear them saying phrases like "I call them the way I see them!", "That's in my genes", "Whomever loves me has to accept me as I am".

Their lack of self-esteem places them in a permanent defensive position and always on high alert, since they don't see anything that pleases them within themselves, they live in perpetual criticism of what they see around them and of people whom they relate to.

The lack of introspection makes them intolerant, perfectionists and demanding to an unreal degree of perfection that never allows them to be satisfied with the actions of others nor with their own. Difficult ones like to keep on the offensive using criticism, verbal aggression and sarcasm as a method of intimidating those they share with.

We could summarize that the difficult ones like to live in fortresses encircled by the ignorance of their transcendent reality, which do not let them enjoy the power of Love that they forgot they had and now do not recognize it. This ignorance leads them to fear and anger when they can't control the world around them to their liking.

How can we deal with these micro-managers of life?

First, knowing that they have no power over you except for the one you confer upon them. Second, realizing they are weak beings with poor self-esteem which do not feel loved nor know how to love.

They tend to attack you preemptively to hide their weakness since they feel worthless and want to tear you down to their level (they use the same preemptive tactic used by many powerful nations!).

If they still persist in their actions in spite of your efforts to love them, as what they most dread is to be ignored, ignore them and go on your way so they remain alone playing with their own biologic excrements!

This behavioral pattern in difficult people (unloved ones) often originates in the programming they received from their family and personal relationships. That's where many powerfully suggestive messages originate, which are subliminally transformed into demanding truths as far as their personality is concerned.

Allow me to give you an example from my own upbringing.

For many years it was suggested to me that I was manually awkward, since I tended to break my own toys and it was difficult for me to learn how to tie my shoes (they didn't know that it was a great excuse for having them tied for me!). The years passed, and when I was halfway through my medical education I was very drawn by the surgical branches, but I was very hesitant about taking this path. This was solved when, rotating through the psychiatry clinics, my group was practicing manual exercises that were used to measure manual skills in children and to my surprise, that day I was the quickest one in carrying them out. I still remember the psychologist's words: "Mr. Figueroa, have you considered becoming a surgeon, since your abilities are superior?" This was enough for me to question my unwarranted fears and aim for a very successful career in the field of pediatric surgery. Was this person perhaps an angel or a messenger of Love in my life?

Carrying on after this example, this ignorance of their own potential leads unloved persons towards fear and anger when they can't control the world around them as they would like it to be. They, the same as so many that condemned Jesus to die on the cross, were the blind of the spirit that could not understand the message of Love that He brought them. From that fact arose the most loving phrase spoken by Jesus in the Bible: "Forgive them, Father, for they know not what they do'" Looking at them with the eyes of the Spirit allowed Him to recognize within them the love they ignored, but which dwelt in them and made them spiritual brothers of Jesus and children of the same Father-Mother.

The great sages of many of the Oriental traditions taught their disciples that these difficult beings sometimes turned to be our best teachers, since they could test our capacity to love, tolerate and forgive.

Sometimes the challenges in our life are the events that stimulate our success. Though I was always an outstanding student in my high school studies, I was never known for my most proper behavior.

In my 3rd year chemistry class I had the misfortune of being in a group with 4 equally unruly guys, which won us the enmity of our teacher, especially when grading our work, which led me to obtain my first "C" ever in a class exam (can you believe it?).

Halfway through the last semester we were given a national aptitude and achievement test whereby I broke the curve in a downward direction. On top of that, when the teacher told me the grade, she said in front of the whole class: "Mr. Figueroa, I don't know what you're going to study but I suggest that it not be anything related to science". Can you imagine how I felt? Interestingly, I accepted it as a challenge which I attacked with all of my energies. I should be noted that from that moment on I got A's in all of my tests and I ended up with a B+ grade point average in the class (the teacher would not give me an A).

What's more, during a participation in a scientific summer camp for students at a local university, I took the same test that I had flunked and it so happens that I got the highest grade in the group. And to finish the story, my grade point average in all of my premed chemistries was A. If you don't believe me I can send you my credit transcript!

Going back to the unloved, it's not easy to deal with these problematic individuals unless our self-esteem has been very strengthened by the clarity of our communication with the transcendent (that we're full of Love), since if we're not, we'll feel threatened by all of the tricks and techniques they will use to intimidate us.

We all have a certain degree of ragged edges in our self-esteem (ask you partner if you don't believe me!), which tends to manifest itself in situations with a lot of emotional pressure, but which we usually control in routine situations in our daily lives. The fearful or spoiled child we all have inside quickly rears up in these difficult situations.

And while meditation yields its effects on the way we view life, what mechanisms can we use in the short term to improve our communication?

The plan of action

The first thing is to think through the mental state we find ourselves in when starting an exchange, by focusing in awareness of where we stand at the time. Does it begin in a state of fear, anger or selfishness in one of the participants?

It's important to know that negative emotional states aggravate the interference of the communicative act, creating a static that muffles the transmission quality. That's why it's important to postpone a dialogue until these feelings have calmed down. This alert state or awareness is one of the goals of meditative practice.

Secondly, we should be aware of our subjectivity and of the endless ways in which we interpret our world. The phrase, "First, know thyself", which originated with ancient Greek schools of philosophy, must set the tone for our communicative action. What is our previous experience with, and our opinion of, the person involved? How has our past experience in childhood influenced our present reaction? (These remain as obsolete but active recordings or programs in our psychological software).

If we have already had negative experiences with this person, our reaction may already be prejudiced by the former, without any validity to justify the present reaction. We must ask ourselves, which are the weaknesses in our personality that could trigger our responses in certain situations? For example, if the person reminds us of an disagreeable experience with an authority figure from our past, we could react to this memory and not to the individual in the present moment. This is the way that many of our spontaneous actions are instinctively programmed.

Man, like the animals, (though sometimes he may not accept himself as such) can be trained to respond to many situations automatically, without being in conscious control of his action. Most advertising and marketing techniques use subliminal suggestion to promote consumption of their products.

Our life experiences continually demonstrate that our initial impression, good or bad, of many persons can change radically after we know them better. If this is true, we must avoid the natural tendency to prejudge our interpretation of the styles of those with whom we already had negative experiences.

The best way to deal with difficult persons is to avoid representing a threatening element for them, like when we surprise them in inappropriate actions, (mistakes) or when we reply to them in the same critical tone in our communications.

"Don't corner the cat that lives in each person, or accept the consequences." The only thing we'll achieve by airing their dirty laundry is an immediate or delayed defensive/aggressive reaction, which in turn generates suffering for both.

Difficult men and women respond to compliments (pious lies), to demonstrations of patience, to rational communication of how their actions affect others and to clarifying questions that help solve the conflict at hand. But if we are not yet ready to seek the gold medal in the Olympic competition with difficult persons, it's better to avoid them and keep on training with meditation! (Remember that there are only two cheeks to receive the blow. Don't hang around so they also whip your behind!)

Open communication is Bidirectional

Open communication implies:

1) Visual and corporal attention – Our eyes and the body must be oriented toward the person addressing us. Don't look around when talking.
2) Body language must reflect openness – avoid crossed arms and legs. Maintain a reasonable distance that does intimidate the person's privacy, especially when discussions heat up!
3) Do not prejudge according to our own biases. We must avoid mentally analyzing, judging or modifying the contents of

what we are hearing, that is, that we must learn to listen. All clarifying questions will wait until the other person finishes communicating. Before challenging a point or criticizing a comment, make clarifying questions regarding what you have perceived (which could be completely opposite to what the other person meant to say). Questions could be like: "I thought I understood... etc., is this impression right?" I interpret your position as being in favor or against such... etc., am I right?"

4) If you feel emotionally affected by the pronouncement, be patient and think of the possibility that the other's intention was not what you think and that you might be mistaken in your interpretation.

5) Remember that we only use 5% of the universal data! Await your turn and explain that you have felt emotionally affected by your interpretation, and allow the person to clarify his or her intention.

6) Always use clear terms to express how you felt by the communication, and never judge the initiator as responsible for what was interpreted by using terms like rude, insensible, liar, male chauvinist, offensive, etc. These terms totally close communication pathways to the rational and objective flow they should have.

7) See with the eyes of the Spirit – When the other party is losing control, look at him as when a child is having a tantrum – don't lower yourself to his level, keep a cordial and low tone of voice, cease intervening, excuse yourself and suggest that the communication may continue later.

8) If there has been any comment that has made you feel offended, don't leave it repressed in the subconscious since you are only hurting yourself. **"Anger is the poison we**

prepare for the person who is offending us, but we drink it ourselves" (unknown source). After the other party has calmed down, tell him how you felt without judging the other party, and allow him to clarify his communication. When communication has completely broken down, one solution to the problem is a private written communication, letting the person know your position and how this break in communication affects both parties. If the person is a loved one, reinforce the love and the importance he has for you in your life. (Please don't nag!)

9) Don't corner the cat that dwells in every man, if we don't want to run away like a dog with its tail between its legs (whoever is without sin, let him cast the first stone). Remember how you have felt when you have made mistakes that have been aired publicly. If we practice what this phrase implies, the range of people who will be our friends) will be innumerable. This practice is one of the most effective ways to practice tolerance and forgiveness in our lives.

No one likes to make mistakes, and especially for them to be made public. A phrase often used in Puerto Rico, "I forgive but never forget", is one of the most frequent reasons behind broken friendships and marriages in the world.

These emotional scars that remain in the memories of the allegedly insulted forestall the reestablishment of open communications that existed in the relationship, where love no longer flows freely.

10) The American saying "Don't rub it in", equivalent to "Don't throw more firewood on a raging fire", is another way of exhibiting an attitude of not forgetting. In Puerto Rico you

could say the equivalent is "I told you so" (Try to remember who used it frequently in your life). Other known and menacing sayings that create this sense of cornering are: "As I was expecting it.", "How many times do I have to tell you?", "¿What more could you expect from him?", etc.

So let's not do to others what we don't want done to ourselves (the Golden Rule) and don't corner the cats in our lives. Remember the Beatles' song: "Let it be, let it be".

Bonus questions to improve your grade (10 points/ question for bookworms)

1) How can we really eliminate the sensation of existential loneliness from our lives?
2) Identify the difficult persons (spiritual lame people) that use you as a crutch in their lives. Identify those you use as crutches in yours.
3) Study and put into practice the 5 qualities of open communications. Keep a log of their application.
4) Give examples of how we can learn to "see with the eyes of the Spirit". (suggestion: look at every being as if it were family: mother, father, sons and brothers)
5) Remember the moments when you were cornered by others. Remember when you cornered others. How did you feel in every situation? Keep your replies for the review of the final exam.

Reflection and Meditation Exercise

Let's review our lives and the mistakes or horrors that we have committed in them. Let's remember those we have wounded one way or another. Let's review the events that culminated in those wounds. Let's remember who gave us a hand in the past and how we felt when they did so. Let's observe how difficult it is to remember sad moments in our lives. What feelings appear when we do it? Can we really erase them from our memory? Did we really have absolute control, and the knowledge and maturity to avoid them at the time? Were we the only ones responsible for the situation? Let's engage in an act of contrition for the events without fixing blame. Let's learn from experience to avoid doing it again.

Let's repeat the visualization from the previous chapter and when we visualize the rainbow bath, focus on where the feelings of guilt for your past mistakes are located and clean those foci with the colors of the force of love and forgiveness. Finally, visualize that infinite multicolored rays beam from the center your heart in all the directions of the universe, reaching the hearts of all we have reviled. Observe how, when you do this, you smile full of happiness. Finally, meditate silently.

CHAPTER VII

TAKING RESPONSIBILITY FOR OUR LIVES AS CO-CREATORS OF OUR UNIVERSES.

The Result of the Final Reconciliation between the Rational Mind and the Transcendent Mind

Glossary, Chapter VII

1) <u>Co-dependence</u>—A psychosocial relationship deemed inappropriate due to the lack of maturity in the parties' behavior. These relationships are established in an addictive and self-destructive way for all the parties, creating suffering for all. A relationship is established whereby a dominant party (perpetrator, co-dependent) and a subjected one (victim, co-dependent) both create a necessity (addictive conduct) with the other. The victim feels that he cannot subsist without the abusive person and the dominant one believes that only he can fulfill the victim's needs. The common denominator for both is the lack of self-esteem and attention (love) that can only seems to be fulfilled only from outside oneself. All sexual abuse relationships, whatever the gender, apply here. Now you know where all of those romantic songs that state that someone cannot live without their beloved come from.

2) <u>Uncertainty Principle</u> – Quantum physics principle established by Dr. Heisenberg, who ascertained in

experiments studying subatomic particles that the observation method affects the experimental results. He was the first one in science to suggest that the observer could change the result of an experiment. In simpler terms, "The observer's viewpoint changes according to the color of the lens (eye of the beholder) with which he observes the universe at that moment".

3) <u>Rational Mind</u> – Left brain hemisphere / World space-time / Son of Man.

4) <u>Transcendent Mind</u> – Right brain hemisphere / Son of God.

5) <u>Spiritually lame (energy vampires)</u> – The dominant person in co-dependent relationships, who uses the dependent partner as a crutch during his or her life's journey.

 The New Man (Self) that rises again from within is reborn in us when we heal the co-dependency relationship of the Creator (God) with His Creation (man) to one of Interdependence and co-responsibility.

If we review the material discussed in chapters V and VI, we will note the emphasis we assign to the confusion originated by:

1) The lack of communication between all parts of the Self: Reason – Love, Knowledge – Wisdom, Science – Spirituality, Rationality – Intuition.

2) The tendency to see the universe exclusively with the rational side, ruled by a tridimensional and temporal viewpoint is what leads men to conclude that they and their surrounding universe are totally independent one from the other, and that the rules that govern this relationship are given only by immutable scientific laws.

This rationalist view of the world creates a persistent unease due to the inability to understand or know what might happen in his immediate future, and leads human beings to accept their lack of permanence and fragility within this scenario. In many cases, this turns life into a survival process of the most resourceful and powerful, akin to that of the animal kingdom.

Thus, his experience leads him to have to accept the reality of sickness, aging and death as inevitable processes that in turn will lead him to try to delay them. (perhaps this gave rise to the discovery of the New World, with Ponce de León seeking the Fountain of Youth, and the successful introduction of Plastic Surgery).

When the Self knows that the time in which he lives and its quality are unpredictable, then he endeavors to search for things that bestow upon him individual happiness at any price, without worrying about the way in which these actions impact everything around him. This vision of individuality leads him to confuse the sensation of feeling loved with the satisfaction of having obtained the achievements and goals he considered necessary to be happy.

Instead of feeling respected for his own worth, he prefers the power of being feared, which he wields like a tyrant, so that all of his relationships provide him his subjective necessities.

As his success, according to the ego (Self), depends only on the individual effort he generates, he does not acknowledge the importance of others' efforts in his achievements, nor does he pity those who cannot imitate his actions. He will therefore never allow himself to be loved, since this action would imply that he would need someone to love him. He thinks that he lives within a protective bubble, where only some beings can penetrate with his permission, as if it were a special privilege for those he allows to do so.

These beings live off of recognition and adulation, because they are like **energy vampires** (spiritually lame) who, without that external energy source, slowly wither.

This extreme individualism, reinforced by how they were raised and by the genetic programming of their DNA, gives rise to the Ego or individual personality, where selfishness originates.

Selfishness, the main reason for humanity's suffering.

These beings never achieve the real satisfaction of feeling loved.

Living, if we go about it selfishly and lacking awareness of our interdependency with the laws of the universe and other beings, turns into a nightmare of suffering with brief moments of happiness. These are the beings that live life as Ricky Martin describes in his song "La Vida Loca".

The search for a way out of this intolerable situation often leads to a nihilist view of life, where individualism and selfishness reign. In the past, this caused some Wise beings to interpret the answer to the questions: Who am I? Where do I come from? and Where am I going? according to their historic, social and geographical situation, and to define transcendence from this point of view, therefore giving birth to the religious concepts that guide us nowadays.

It would seem that these great Wise men, who guided men in their first steps in the process of civilization and the development of the social interaction that is so needed for an appropriate coexistence, started ever so carefully giving man this information, in small bites, digestible according to man's capacity. To better understand this, review the chapter on the great universal broadcaster and interferences in communication.

The problem that arose later and that still affects humanity is sectarian intolerance, which originated most of the wars and social repressions by trying to establish one [belief] as the true or superior one over the other.

Man's co-dependent relationship with God

Due to the communication's error established between the individual interpretation of the Creator (transcendent) and the individual interferences of its creation (man), broadly discussed in chapter IV, and encouraged by the hierarchical structures of all religions, man developed a type of pathological (abnormal) co-dependency relationship with the "divinity" that, in many cases, and paradoxically, did not alleviate humanity's suffering.

As we discussed previously, these co-dependent relationships are characterized by an addictive reliance upon another person or belief where in order to feel happy, one needs the person who "completes" his or her "seeming" deficiencies.

This is the origin of many religious factions that have populated our history!

Characteristics of Co-Dependent People:
Low self-esteem
Repressed (inhibited)
Compulsive
Manipulative (controlling)
Confused and delusional
Dependent
Insecure and weak in expressing their needs
Lacking confidence

The misinterpretation of this relationship can lead man to feel a sense of guilt and confusion, to view the world as a "valley of tears" where his role consists of accepting being a "victim" of the experience of suffering as something "deserved" and inevitable, where his only solution is handing over all of his autonomy and decision-making power to the concept of the Creator and the religious structure that will assure his "salvation" from his valley of tears.

The system originated from this relationship offers some guarantees some rewards if you follow certain rules of life and penalties if these rules are broken. Though this common relationship is not the reality for every human being, there will always be a degree of co-dependency between man and the image of "his God", which will result in several degrees of co-dependent manifestation.

Religious skepticism could arise as a result of this relationship. Atheists, though courageous in their challenges based on scientific materialism, separate themselves from all metaphysical processes. You have to admire that, nonetheless, they manage to establish ethical life relationships based on the respect for their humanity.

Healing the co-dependent relationship and creating an interdependent one

The way out from this co-dependent relationship lies in man's capacity to understand that his relationship with his Creator is one of shared responsibilities (co-responsibility). In other words, there's an interdependency between the Creator and his creation. Science, as I have already explained, tells us that we are tridimensional manifestations in time and space (matter) and that we originated from the transcendent nature of linear no-time and space (antimatter).

To understand this you must refer to chapter I, where we explained that the Universe and ourselves (like a microcosm of the former) are 95% imperceptible, timeless beings and 5% perceptible temporal ones, where the subjective experience of life depends on the intentional vision of our free will. Also, we must remember our true origins and understand that the experience of life is a single one, where the transcendent manifests in an infinite and changing range of possibilities, and where the interdependence between its opposites (matter/ antimatter, son of God/son of Man, relative mind/absolute mind, microcosm/macrocosm, left brain hemisphere/right brain hemisphere, etc.) is inevitable.

Our left brain hemisphere (material mind) which gives rise to the Ego, makes us afraid and reinforces our co-dependent viewpoint, generating our individualistic state and encouraging us to forget that the source of all this suffering is the ignorance of our true origins or nature. This hemisphere reinforces that we only are what is born and dies, which came from our parents' DNA.

That mind that encourages our Ego (rational mind) is also responsible for the tendency to project human features upon the Universe's creative force, where man, which should be made in the image and likeness of the Creator, contaminates the true image of his Creator, by defining Him according to man's own human limitations. We can find that tendency in almost every way of describing God in most sacred books of all Western and Eastern civilizations.

Our right brain hemisphere (transcendent mind) supports us in acknowledging our infinite potential when we understand our true nature and origins, and the importance of our free will. The latter gives us the ability to choose to live like an interdependent whole, within which, we are as musical notes inside a great symphony or the various shades of color in a painting, where our role is as important as that of every component but not better than any other. Meditate a long while on this sentence!

This feeling of interdependency makes us responsibly share our role in that universe and our responsibility in its co-creation. The right hemisphere or spiritual mind makes us feel that we are a part of "something" before birth and that we return to that "something" when we die. It makes us feel immortal and a part of a broader evolutionary process than that of our limited earthly experience of living in time and space.

The Co-creation of the Universe is originated by the interdependent action of the transcendent (God, Love) and its creation (Universe and man)

In the Chinese Taoist tradition, the universe was divided into two parts: Yang (Heaven) (masculine) and Yin (Earth) (feminine), where man was a balanced manifestation of both, found between Heaven and Earth. From the sacred books of the Christian tradition I infer that though the Kingdom of God was not of this world, it dwelled in the heart of all men. I speculate this by interpreting the following scriptures from John 18:36 where Jesus answered: "My Kingdom is not an earthly kingdom. If it were, my followers would fight to keep me from being handed over to the Jewish leaders. But my Kingdom is not of this world" and Luke 17:20-21: "Now when He was asked by the Pharisees when the kingdom of God would come, He answered them and said, 'The kingdom of God does not come with observation; nor will they say, 'See here!' or 'See there!' For indeed, the kingdom of God is within you." Maybe the message intended or implied was rather a question of recognizing that the potential characteristic of his kingdom resided within each one of us, in order to be able to recognize it later in all of our brethren.

The Christ or Wise man is that which, though living with his feet on the ground, always keeps his sight on the Heavens.

 Man's Free Will: a gift of Love and Tolerance from God to Man

In order to understand this new interdependent relationship of Man with God, we must try to establish a less tainted vision of Him, without projecting upon that nature the human characteristics that tend to limit its true potential. To achieve it, let's see how some oriental traditions described this divine nature, and how the sacred Judeo-Christian books did the same thing.

In the Taoist tradition, as well as in the Buddhist, divine nature was bestowed an indefinable character to avoid its distortion by the interpretation of the self. The Tao Te Ching, referring to that which originates Yang (Qi) (energy from heaven), says:

"The Tao that can be spoken is not the eternal Tao. The name that can be named is not the eternal name. The nameless is what is eternally real. Naming is what gives birth to Heaven and Earth (particularities)."

We already mentioned that, in the Old Testament, though there are a myriad of names or qualities with which to name God, there is only one, unpronounceable, which gives origin to the rest:

"That whose Name is so immensely large that it will not fit in my mouth." And finally, when Moses asks the burning bush and demands from God, "Who are you?", God replies:

"I am what I am."

All the previous phrases imply that:

The origin of everything that is known is a potential state without preexisting characteristics, from whence all possible manifestations arise, but only when there is an observer to perceive them.

The cognitive interpretation of that original state is totally subjective and prejudiced, depending on the observer's ability (historical, religious and philosophical discrepancies).

The Tremendous Shared Responsibility that Arises from the Co-creation of Man in the Universe.

We already know that there is no limit to the possibilities of how the transcendent state can manifest, since it is as changeable as the amount of observers viewing it.

It would seem that the divinity is a facilitating (loving) nature of creation, which depends on the creative intention of man's individual free will, and its manifestation in our time and space reality (material universe).

The kingdom of the Spirit is a potential state with infinite possibilities, and the material universe is one of realities co-created by the mind of man, according to the laws of the universe. Isn't that what Love does in the Universe?

Isn't Love the great facilitator of the Universe's creation according to the free will of man's mind which, if facilitated by a selfish being generates a hell, and by a loving being, a paradise?

The Origin of Evil and Suffering is based on the Ignorance of whom we are: "Forgive them, Father, for they know not what they do."

Actions based on selfishness arise from the lack of recognition of our true origin (Love) which potentially lies within every Son of Man (self), though he may not acknowledge it yet. This lack of recognition turns us into the blind in Spirit or spiritual lame men that create the need to use others as crutches, creating an addictive co-dependency to seek happiness.

All of the universe that exists in the three dimensions of time, space and distance is ruled by scientific laws. One of the most important ones is Newton's Third Law, "When one body exerts a force on a second body, the second body simultaneously exerts a force equal in magnitude and opposite in direction to that of the first body". It tells us that if a body "A" exerts an action upon another body "B", the latter applies to "A" another action which is equal in force and in the opposite direction. That is, that every action in our world generates a proportional response (reaction) to the initial one. We can summarize that every cause has a specific effect in our universe (remember the interdependency of everything in the universe?).

If we review everything said up to now, you can deduct that everything that exists, that is measurable and visible is manifested due to the creative action of the mind, which originates from the Creator's (Love) or indefinable potential state. Yet it's the final way of manifesting will depend on the intention or free will of the individual's mental action.

If the self identifies itself as a transitory, individual self, independent of its environs, it will follow the painful path of suffering and the fruitless and unceasing quest for material happiness. But if the self recognizes its true legacy as a son of the Spirit, it applies the phrase: When the Self learns to observe the Universe through the eyes of the Spirit, it perceives only Love.

Let's remember that the Universe, in tis densest manifestation in time and space, is composed of identical subatomic energy particles that arranged themselves in families of elements in the Periodic Table, differing between each other only in the amount and arrangement of the particles. It is these subtle changes in configuration the ones that manifest the final and dramatic differences between lead and gold!

Might these variables in the elements be the influence of quantum physics' Uncertainty Principle, which posits that every observable thing is influenced by the subjective mental state of the observer? Then we'd have to accept that the mind is the one that organizes and classifies this universe of endless possibilities into those that are akin to the observer's subjective experience. We could speculate that our biological DNA (Son of Man) is programmed with its 5 senses to understand this Universe of time and space.

That would be the extension of Einstein's law of time relativity to the relativity of everything that exists in the space defined by time.

It would then imply that if time is a relative phenomenon, every manifestation occurring within time should be relative too.

From this realization we could conclude: That every experience regarding how we see and understand our mini universes (co-creations) will be relative and subjective in reference to our genetic program or heredity, to the programming we have learned in our individual experience of interacting with the external world, and to the agreement with others in the way that we interpret the experience of living habits and values.

In this way man builds a social and psychological (personality) entity that differentiates him according to the geographical, socioeconomic, racial and religious environment in which he develops. Always remember that though we all agree in the quest for happiness, we'll never be able to agree on how to find it. That's why we must be very careful with what we think, and remember Buddha's words:

"The thought manifests in the spoken word.
The word manifests in an action.

The action develops into a habit.
The habit solidifies in the character.
Destiny arises from the character.
So watch your thoughts carefully
And allow them to arise from love,
Which itself arises from respect towards all beings"

We could add, "not from selfishness, which arises from the denial of the Love that is within you."

From all of the above we must understand the importance of the way in which we judge everything that surrounds us, because we will be co-responsible for what we have co-created with our thoughts. Let's learn to see the Universe through the eyes of Love and not by the selfishness that engenders suffering.

The Ego, The Thief that Steals Happiness from Our Hearts

The man who lives an earthly experience resembles the prince that was kidnapped as a child during a war, and is raised as a slave by his captors, and who lives with the hope of regaining the state of abundance that he carries as a long-lost remembrance in his heart.

Even though he is later freed, there is no material reward that will fill the void he carries in his heart. It will take until someone who knows the kingdom whence he came, and remembers the beautiful things that he had, to help him acknowledge his true heritage and origin. Then he will embark on a search for his lost Kingdom.

In this case our kidnapper represents our own Ego, created by the material mind where, along with fear and ignorance, it imprisons us in the hermetic prison of time and space where we are born. There we alternate between incessant transitory times of happiness and suffering, with the inevitable reality of aging and death.

When the Prince (Son of Man) lets himself be loved by all of those who acknowledged in him his true heritage (Son of God), he begins to recall his origins and embarks on the search for whom he really is, where he comes from and where he is headed.

That's why the way to elicit human beings' greatness is by loving them intensely without preconceived expectations. That's another thing that, if we learn and apply it, guarantees passing the final test of life!

Love Always Offers, with a Special Supersized Combo, Forgiveness Along with the Act of Sin.

To understand the above, we must remember that the transcendent state of no time (Love) in the Universe exists in a virtual state without preconceived qualities, where the Self generates with his mind a corresponding state of happiness (paradise) or unhappiness (hell), and that selfish actions arise from ignorance of the Self's true nature, where evil or wickedness comes from the ignorance of the existence of Goodness (Love).

This implies that every loving or selfish action, according to the Newtonian law of correspondence, generates a similar and proportional response towards the being that starts it and the one that perceives it, and this only happens in experiences within time and space, without affecting the transcendent world of no time and space ("he whose name is so large it will not fit in my mouth" "God").

This realization would put us at theological odds within the Judeo-Christian tradition, since it would be an impossibility to sin against the transcendent nature or God (remember that God is pure Love, who does not understand how the Ego judges his universe). Our selfish actions would affect mainly our brothers in our earthly experience; the sons of Man. This would imply that, if there were a need to ask forgiveness from somebody, it would rather be from the one we caused to suffer: the son of Man.

The most loving act in the universal matrix (God-Love) is to bestow free will upon the Self so he can use the qualities of reason (left hemisphere) in balance with the qualities of his Heart (right hemisphere). This allows him to live in interdependence and solidarity with his brothers according to the golden rule that says, "Do not do unto others what you would not want done to yourself" and "Do unto others what you would want done to yourself".

Then we must ask, where does Divine justice lay, if there isn't someone or something that judges the consequences of our actions? When sharing our Universe's experience of time and space, all of our thoughts and actions (conscious and unconscious) generate a corresponding action under Newton's law of Action and Reaction (cause and effect), which results consequences from these. These are what Oriental traditions, who believe in the experience of reincarnation, call individual and group Karma. I prefer to call it the law of Love, since it allows the Universe, co-created by the sons of God, to correct mistakes created by ignorance of its Ego (son of Man) without individual punitive connotations!

Same as when the Universe records or registers in its memory every action in the energy realm, it also records the individual actions of beings that populate it. We could speculatively postulate that, as we will later discuss, since there is a DNA that registers the history of the organism's biological experience, there must be a spiritual DNA that records the experience of the transcendental Self and processes the information learned from individual and group experiences in the life of the Universe. **This cause-effect relationship between each mental or physical action and its result does not imply any incriminating process, independent of the experience in and of itself.**

The only thing that guides this process is the quest for balance (Love) in the totality of the individual and the unbalancing action of the Ego.

We could compare the act of sin as a selfish action, conscious or unconscious, of a human being upon another (the other). **This act generates suffering, but never affects the Universe's Love-generating matrix (God). Therefore Man "sins" against the sons of Man, but not against God.**

And this free will of mental and physical action, and the consequences of these actions, are the most compassionate form of Love, giving each individual a way to redeem his actions and allowing him to live the consequences.

That's why I said that with every act of sin comes, in a combo pack, the option of Forgiveness to redeem it.

For those of you that follow the Judeo-Christian and Muslim tradition, and see the earthly experience as unique and individual, the justice of human beings' selfish actions will be decided in a final judgment, where the "Soul" of some that have followed the infinite religious rules of each tradition will be compensated by an "eternal" experience of happiness and joy in Heaven, or of "eternal" suffering in Hell.

For those of you that feel close to the concept of reincarnation, the impersonal law of cause and effect (Karma) seems to result in repeated life experiences, which according to their previous actions will lead to various degrees of happiness or suffering, that could represent the sensation of living in heaven or hell in that experience.

What worse hell than the experiences we have read about in the history of what men have done and still do to their neighbors on Earth? Where has divine justice been in all the wars that have been justified to impose or preach a religious belief over a different belief?

But even those who believe in the concept of reincarnation are not totally right, since as I previously said, "We must remember our true origin and realize that the experience of life is only one, where the transcendent manifests in an infinite and changing range of possibilities, and where the interdependence of one with another is inevitable, which gives rise to the true solidarity of our humanity in this experience". 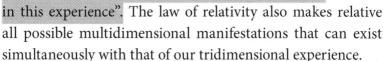 The law of relativity also makes relative all possible multidimensional manifestations that can exist simultaneously with that of our tridimensional experience.

Quantum physics suggests that all possibilities that we could experience and interpret as linear sequences of lives and incarnations are actually occurring simultaneously, but our temporal individual consciousness only allows us to see one of those multiple experiences! Recent scientific string or super-string theories suggest an infinite additional number of dimensions that surround us and which we cannot see nor understand.

Therefore, reincarnation is an experience of the Ego, co-created by its ignorance, by not realizing that what reincarnates in the universe is God (Love) through his Sons, in an infinite multidimensional experience! (If you understand this, you already passed the final exam.)

I prefer to assume my co-responsibility in the creation of my experience, be it linear or multidimensional, making my small contribution towards the harmony of the great symphony of the Universal experience. We must equally break away from the co-dependent state where the Ego binds us, exchanging it for a relationship of interdependence and solidarity with the Universe and its infinite manifestations.

And now, my companions on the path of life, let's share that path in brotherhood, looking at the Universe through the eyes of the Spirit.

Bonus questions to improve your grade (10 points/ question for bookworms)

1) Let's study the concept of co-dependence in our lives carefully, and search for this type of relationship in our upbringing, that of our children and in our romantic and business relationships. Let's observe how they have affected us and how we can correct them. Suggestions: look for your failures, fears, your failed relationships, your dysfunctional upbringings, your resentments and your experiences with the difficult persons in your lives.

2) How can we use what we learned about co-responsibility (free will) and co-creativity to correct the harmful aspects of co-dependent relationships in our lives?

3) Examine every action that has generated guilt and suffering in your lives, evaluate the concept of forgiveness and the causal law of Love upon these actions. Ask yourselves: Whom do you harm? Why did you do it? Who judges and decides the consequence of the action? How can you correct it as quickly as possible? Must we demand forgiveness for the actions that others have made us suffer for in our lives? Use the wise words of the Master Jesus, "Forgive them, for they know not what they do", and apply them to your selves and to others in your apprenticeship in the school of life.

Practical Exercise

Besides continuing with the previously recommended meditations, let's make an effort to carry over the meditative state to daily life by means of a state of alert, whereby we maintain our vision through the eyes of the Spirit. Let's practice the human qualities of Love, patience, empathy, tolerance, compassion, happiness, joy and courage (perseverance) to conserve them in the face of attacks from our Ego. Use the previously suggested techniques for communications with the unloved (difficult persons), first starting with your loved ones and then extending their reach as you master the previous phase. Never forget to allow yourselves to be loved every moment, because the purest source of Love is found in you!

CHAPTER VIII

RETURN TO THE GARDEN OF EDEN:
REMEMBERING THE WAY HOME.

The Map and Compass that Facilitate Our Return

Glossary, Chapter VIII

1) <u>Compassionate Intelligence</u>—When Love guides reason in the certainty of a holographic and supportive universe, the loving wisdom that characterized all of the great masters appears. These Masters learned to live in the world without being of the world, because they recognized that their heart always dwelt in the Kingdom of God.

Remembering the Way Back to Our True Home

If we examine chapter III, we find that there are certain inherent and forgotten qualities with which we must re-connect in order to remember the way back to our home and to reestablish the existence of the following abilities:

1) The ability to understand your origin.
2) The ability to understand how they interact.
3) The ability to understand how these influence your view of life (happiness or suffering).

After the Self acknowledges the existence of these abilities, the desire to seek to return to our home and to find a way to guide us in that journey is born, something that we will discuss here.

The Garden of Eden: significance of the Myth in our life

It's the myth of how primordial Love gives rise to:

- Mental duality and the appearance of what exists, time and the infinite cycles associated with it.
- The appearance of emotions and judgment of what exists due to the attachment to goodness and avoidance of evil, that generates Ego and results in the disappearance of innocence.
- The state in which the self's awareness found itself in this place was described by ancient religions (AC) and by the Christian one as a purer one, nearest to the "creative" nature of the universe, which was named "Heaven" by many religious traditions.

The Garden of Eden: the Symbolic significance

1) Represents the Golden Age where the self lived in a state of innocence with minimal mental dualism, and was almost in the presence of the creative Divinity. It still did not distinguish good from evil.
2) The tree of forbidden fruit – potential state of knowledge of good and evil. Represents reason, rational intelligence and the development of the 5 senses that allow the self to organize the universe in apparently immutable laws

according to their interpretation (the universe of matter-time-space). The son of man begins to co-create with his free will. Continually messing up things since then!

3) The apple – represents the capacity to analyze, judge, and classify the world into good, bad and indifferent (the rational mind of the ego). It's the development of the 5 senses to their maximum capacity, with the consequence (responsibility) of experiencing pleasure and suffering. The emergence of intelligence, reason and analysis, and the capacity to order the universe in laws created by its mind (habits and customs) represents the loss of innocence (irresponsibility?), and the emergence of time and the cycles of birth, sickness and death. Where did the saying of, "an apple a day keeps the doctor away keeps the doctor away", come from?

4) The Tree of Life – Represented the immortal nature of the self that understands that time does not exist. This is the state of Wisdom that potentially exists in each Son of Man when he realizes that he is a Son of God and that he can manifest in his universal experience in Love, as the Son of God, the Christ or the Buddha.

5) It's the last part of the cosmic path, when the prodigal son returns to the house of his Father, with the acquired wisdom of his earthly experience!

The Self's Two Inheritances

The Prodigal Son – (The Son of Man) – All of us which have to this world are as prodigal sons. We ask for our inheritance, intelligence and reason, to use it appropriately in the universe, but we forget our true inheritance and dedicate ourselves to living, as the song goes, "La Vida Loca" (thoughtless life). This is the person that lives in selfishness. "Living, if we do it selfishly and lacking awareness of our interdependence with the laws of the universe and other beings, turns into a nightmare of suffering with brief moments of happiness".

The son of God (of the Spirit) – This represents every being that leaves the house of this father (the Garden of Eden) with a clear awareness of this true heritage, which is the spiritual lineage based on Love and the primordial state of the universe.

This is the self that learns to look through the eyes of the Spirit and only sees Love around itself.

But the only way to learn this wise viewpoint is by living the earthly experience! (If you learn it you also pass the final exam!)

Those who learned this lesson turned into the great Masters of all the religions, such as Jesus, Buddha, Hermes, Moses, Krishna, Lao-Tzu, Mohammed, etc...

What, then, does the Return to the Garden of Eden represent?

1) It's the mental act of remembering what we have forgotten.
2) It's the act of re-encountering our two natures (reconciliation, connection or communion).
3) It's the act of learning to look at the universe anew without judgment or preconception (looking with the eyes of the spirit).
4) It's the act of forgiving ourselves and others.
5) It's the act of meditation (open communication or communion).

Which map must we use to return to paradise?

It's built out of a series of attitudes and actions that help us find the way.

First we have to accept the fact that we are lost. Paradoxically, science helps us with this. This is the only prerequisite to take this class.

To use the compass that will always guide us in our path which is meditation and prayer.

On the way back we'll meet many good Samaritans (the Teachers of the School of Life) that have already walked the path, and who will help us to keep on the right track.

Science and Reason

Science is what helps us find our origin when it teaches us, for example, through the previous observations which we have already discussed, that "Earthly life is a mirage created by the thirst of individualism".

Examining what has been discussed, science suggests that 95% of the universe is invisible (antimatter). And that the perceptible 5% (matter) is where we believe we live. Science can only understand and research this very small part. We previously discussed the scientific theories that suggest the existence of many more dimensions beyond the three that we are aware of.

And therefore time was a fictitious creation of our minds (Einstein's relativity theory).

We previously postulated that everything that is perceptible is a temporal manifestation of the imperceptible. Some examples are wind, light, thoughts, art, music, the subatomic particles of matter, etc. And that in the same way that we are beings that originate from an immortal nature (outside time and space) that transiently manifest ourselves in time. If you still don't understand this, you will definitely flunk the final exam!

The Compass, the Instrument that Facilitates Communication and Meditation.

1) It leads to a re-encounter between our two natures at the negotiating table (our heart).
2) The Ego initially fights like a cornered cat, embracing the 5 senses because it's afraid to lose its control, because it's the source of his adopted sons, the unloved ones. Those selfish people who don't really know what they are doing but believe they know everything! Patience, patience…
3) When the two types of minds meet at the negotiating table, it's as if an orphan child finds his lost mother and vice versa. Remember the feeling recalled in the song "Love is more wonderful the second time around".
4) The relative (material) mind is like a record in repeat mode, that repeats the same message to us incessantly and that does not let us listen to the true beautiful melody that dwells in our hearts.
5) Then we shall finally know that we have arrived at the Garden of Eden when the self learns to see the universe through the eyes of the Spirit and finds only Love.

The Teachers (Good Samaritans)

These are the good Samaritans that, after having found the way, return to help others find theirs. They give us support and hope in those moments when we falter.

They have obtained **Compassionate Intelligence** because their experience in the universe of duality has awoken their forgotten compassion. This compassion is the Christian and Buddhist quality that the great masters have asked us to emulate.

When we arrive at and remember our true nature, it feels like we have always being an integral part of something greater, and are not really only individuals independent from our common source and its creation.

Feeling part of a great spiritual family lets us understand clearly the phrase, "Love thy neighbor as thyself".

Compassionate Intelligence is when love guides reason to the definite realization of our holographic and supportive universe. It's the origin of this loving wisdom which characterized all of the great masters. These Masters learned to live in the world like visiting foreign diplomats, since they acknowledged that their heart always dwell in their country of origin, the Kingdom of God.

They always lived by keeping their feet on the ground, without averting their eyes from heaven.

The origin of religious discrepancies.

Religious discrepancies originate due to the subjective limitations of the 5 senses and communications problems arising from them, and never based on the teachings from the great Samaritans, but rather on our interpretations of those teachings.

Remember that the divinity (the unifying transcendent force of the universe) is the great Universal broadcaster, that only broadcasts Love without obstacles or favorites.

And never forget the phrase from the Jewish Cabala, "The Name of God is so immensely large, that it will not fit in my mouth."

The Power of Thought, Faith and Love

Thought moves the universe's energy, where results depend on the intentions of the thinker. The more the ego involves itself (with its individual desires), the worse it is. **The best intention is a loving one, which directs its intention without intent!** (Don't worry, I'll explain this in another book about healing).

Intention is more effective when the spiritual wisdom is more evolved (awareness of solidarity).

The internal wisdom (Son of God) in our self is the true pilot of our cosmic spaceship, and not the ego.

Faith is the passively active act of allowing the reconciliation of our dual nature, very similar to religious communion.

Negative emotions are like energy scars that obstruct the free circulation of our spiritual energy.

Arriving at the Garden of Eden. How shall we know we have arrived?

When you arrive at the Garden of Eden, life takes on a flavor so delicious that all experiences taste equally good. We also obtain all the positive qualities that Love generates. We stop criticizing the world manifests and only dedicate ourselves to help others who have not yet remembered the way home.

And then, when we look at our backyard (heart), we realize that we never abandoned the Garden of Eden!

Bonus questions to improve your grade (10 points/ question for bookworms)

1) I want you to analyze the reason why God placed the tree of knowledge of good and evil in the garden in the first place, if he did not want his children to eat its fruit. I'd love to hear your answers!

2) What are the requirements to find (create) our map?

3) Why do we say that Faith is a passively active act? Why doesn't everything that we create with our minds instantly become a reality in our lives? How are priorities established in God's universal waiting list, in order to grant his children's desire?

4) List what you believe are the qualities of the Great Masters. ¿Do you believe that you could mimic them at some time?

5) Describe in your own words what "Compassionate Intelligence" means to you. Seek opportunities to apply it in your lives. Give examples of some of them. Is this form of acting compatible with the present business system? Mention forms of government that have tried to use Compassionate Intelligence in their political systems.

6) Remember some of the good Samaritans that have given you to drink in your life's journey. Do you recall how these actions affected you? have you repeated these actions with others?

Exercise in meditation and reflection

In order to remember our origins, we must learn to see how we look and how we must look at the rest of the Universe through the eyes of the Spirit. To that end I have adapted this meditation from the Buddhist tradition to our Christian viewpoint.

A Colorful Bath of Love

Seated in a comfortable position with our back straight and our head held up high, let's visualize a source of spiritual strength or energy that makes us feel protected. For example, the figure of the Sacred Heart of Jesus, young-looking, smiling and standing, with open arms and beaming rays of multicolored light from the center of His heart to ours, in which a small seed exists.

Let's understand the meaning of the exercise. Jesus represents the human manifestation of the Holy Spirit which is the force of Love that God left us after his Son left. The multicolored rays represent the infinite ways in which Love can manifest among us. The seed in our heart represents the latent form in which that Love dwells in man.

As those rays of light fill our heart, let us feel ourselves loved and protected by the Love of God and let's observe how the small seed starts to open and in turn irradiates the multiple colors of Love in all directions. Initially, let's imagine that those colors bathe us in love and penetrate every part of our bodies, especially those where there is a discomfort, and let's see how the latter is soothed and healed.

After we have been filled with happiness and wellness, we're going to share this with all human beings, especially with those who have hurt us due to their ignorance of love.

Let's visualize that multicolored rays emerge from our heart towards all human beings without distinction, including those who have left this physical world, and those that, in our thoughts, have brought suffering to our lives. Let's dedicate some minutes to this action and then let's rest our mind in silence for a few more minutes. Let's finish by giving thanks for this opportunity. Let's do this exercise ever day upon waking and when going to sleep.

Finally, to keep our mind in a peaceful state, let's imagine that our thoughts are as clouds in the sky and that our natural peaceful state is like the blue color in the sky. Let our thoughts pass like clouds, without following them, focusing on the blue of the sky, our natural state.

CHAPTER IX

FINAL EXAM FOR THE DROPOUTS IN THE SCHOOL OF LIFE

INSTRUCTIONS: CHOOSE THE BEST ANSWER AMONG THE OPTIONS.

1) What is antimatter?

   a) A new socialist party that opposes unchecked consumerism
   b) What science says gave birth to matter
   c) That which occupies the greater part of our universe (72%)
   d) What ghosts are made of

2) In what percentage of our potential universe do we perceive that we exist?

   a) Most of us in none!
   b) In 5%
   c) In 95%
   d) None of the above

3) Einstein's relativity theory could explain the following:

   a) Puerto Ricans habit of arriving late for appointments!
   b) Why we never have time to finish work assigned by the boss!
   c) Why we see the graduates of our high school class as older than ourselves!
   d) Why time changes its measurement depending on where it is measured in the universe

4) The phrase "I think, therefore I am" was coined by:

   a) Plato in the Republic
   b) Isaac Newton in his theory of Mechanical Physics
   c) Rene Descartes in his theory of Rationalism
   d) None of the above

5) The phrase "I am, therefore I think" was coined by:

   a) Plato
   b) Einstein
   c) Isaac Newton
   d) Ivan Figueroa, M.D.

6) The self's holographic effect within his universe is acknowledged in:

   a) The Biblical quotes "What you will do to the smallest of my people, I shall deem you did for me" y "Love thy neighbor as thyself."
   b) Global warming associated with atmospheric pollution caused by man
   c) Genetic alteration of agricultural products
   d) All of the above

7) The Golden Law:

   a) Classified the value of money based on the planet's gold reserves
   b) Fixes the price of gold based on its weight
   c) Do not do unto others what you would not want done to yourself
   d) Rich people always get their way!

8) What are the highlights of co-creative responsibility?

   a) Free will makes us co-responsible for the result of our actions
   b) The most efficient way to manifest God's Love in the universe is through each son of God's (man) co-responsible action
   c) The earth is our home and whatever affects it affects all of its sons
   d) All of the above

9) We can state the following about our DNA:

    a) It came from monkeys
    b) Each race arose from a different one
    c) It came from the stars and it's the one that gave birth to all races
    d) None of the above

10) The law of the conservation of energy:

    a) Promotes a reduction in the exaggerated consumption of oil
    b) Promotes adulterating gasoline with alcohol to avoid alcoholism
    c) Forces me to use regular gasoline instead of Premium
    d) Is the law of thermodynamics that affirms that neither energy nor matter can be lost in the universe since one transforms into the other

11) Qualities that characterize selfish people:

    a) They act independently of their effects on others
    b) They propitiate individualism as opposed to interdependence
    c) They live without transcendence, since their existence ends with the death of the body
    d) All of the above

12) The only thing that human beings agree on is:

   a) That we like vegetarian cuisine
   b) That we all want to be happy
   c) That we want to be U.S. citizens
   d) That we'll all go to heaven

13) What did Jesus imply on the cross when he said, "Father, forgive them, for they know not what they do" when referring to those that were killing them?

   a) They did not acknowledge Jesus as the Son of God
   b) They did not acknowledge that they were also children of God
   c) They did not acknowledge that they were Jesus' spiritual brethren
   d) All of the above

14) Cosmic Schizophrenia is:

   a) A new form of mental disease that affects astronauts that spend a lot of time in space
   b) What happens to astronauts when they eat a lot of junk food in space
   c) What they undergo when mission control tells them that they don't have enough fuel to return to Earth
   d) The mental confusion where the Self manifests a dual personality, as son of God or son of Man, that makes him live in an unbalanced universe and which produces much confusion and suffering

15) Shamata is:

a) A meditation time-killing technique
b) A mortal blow with a Samurai sword
c) A form of meditation with one eye closed and the other one open
d) None of the above

16) What are the interferences that prevent man from recognizing the totality of his reality?

a) The limitation of perceiving the universe with his 5 senses
b) His genetic heritage
c) Habits and prejudices learned during our upbringing
d) All of the above

17) What are the mistakes that can happen receiving the signal from the Great Broadcaster?

a) The interference in each person's individual interpretation (radio) due to his individual experiences (upbringing, education, race, etc.)
b) Choosing the wrong station with his free will (hard rock instead of salsa!)
c) The interferences created when retransmitting the message received to others
d) All of the above

18) The periodic table is:

   a) A numerical reference to calculate the duration of the menstrual cycle
   b) What industry uses for periodically calculating employee firings!
   c) The way in which Mendeleev classified the elements in family groups with similar chemical characteristics
   d) None of the above

19) We can state that habits and learned conduct patterns are:

   a) Good when we like them and bad when we don't like them
   b) Relative to our upbringing, race, nationality, social status, religious beliefs and genetic inheritance
   c) The main cause of our social, political and personal conflicts
   d) All of the above

20) The true source of suffering is:

   a) Humanity's social and economic inequality
   b) Extreme capitalism
   c) Political corruption in governments
   d) The void (lack of solidarity) that originates within us (cosmic schizophrenia) when we don't recall our true origin and the true power of the use of free will with love

21) The source of evil is due to:

   a) The Ego's ignorance in not recognizing its origins in Love (God)
   b) The fear that arises from the possibility of aging, getting sick and dying which springs from ignorance, and the frustration, envy and anger (wrath) that arises from the fact that we cannot avoid these life events
   c) Selfish actions that lead the self to fulfill his individual needs first, without caring for the consequences to others
   d) All of the above

22) We can state that free will:

   a) Is the same for everyone
   b) Only happens in democratic countries
   c) Was invented by George Washington
   d) Is the gift of love that enables us to co-create with co-responsibility

23) The first step towards passing life's final exam is understanding these abilities:

   a) The ability to understand your origins
   b) The ability to understand how they interact
   c) The ability to understand how these influence his view of life (happiness or suffering)
   d) All of the above

24) Which of the following is the most effective quality in order to achieve a loving co-responsible co-creative act?

a) Intelligence
b) Persistence
c) Prayer
d) Patience

25) Faith is:

a) An act of loving co-dependency in the creative force
b) A prayer based on certainty of the creative force that dwells outside us
c) An extreme reliance in the ability of Love to rule the universe in its own way (like Frank Sinatra)
d) An act of loving and patient co-responsible co-creation (it knows how to wait for its turn in the universe's waiting list)

26) What does the "Prodigal Son" parable teach us about the "nagging" that we use with our children?

a) That nobody learns through others' experiences
b) That for the Father, the spiritual heritage is worth more than the material one
c) That we, same as the prodigal son, will learn to acknowledge our true heritage through life's hardships
d) All of the above

27) We can state about religions:

    a) That they all have part of the truth
    b) That none has all of the truth
    c) That they make the mistake of making God in their image and likeness
    d) All of the above

28) What might man use from escape from the prison of being born, aging and dying that he built with his 5 senses?

    a) The drill of Love and Faith
    b) The drill of free will and co-responsibility
    c) The drill of meditation
    d) All of the above

29) Meditation is:

    a) A passive action that is carried out using some very uncomfortable positions
    b) The repetition of some sounds in strange languages
    c) A bidirectional open communications act, expressing yourself and listening
    d) None of the above

30) To sit the Ego at the negotiating table (heart) you have to:

a) Force it
b) Fool him with promises of rewards and power in its life
c) Convince it with reason and the example of experiences and actions
d) All of the above

31) The worst punishment we can inflict on a Latino in his communication act is:

a) To call him "Hispanic" in a racial sense
b) To tell him he has no rhythm when dancing
c) Tie down his two arms and force him to describe the last soccer game he saw
d) None of the above

32) Some synonyms for the difficult people in our lives are:

a) Blind in spirit
b) Unloved
c) Spiritually lame
d) All of the above

33) What relationships do all difficult people like to establish with others?

a) Totalitarian
b) Support
c) Co-dependency
d) Interdependence

34) What are the most outstanding characteristics of difficult people?

    a) Poor self-esteem
    b) They hide their weakness with preemptive abusive attacks
    c) They don't know how to love or let themselves be loved
    d) All of the above

35) Why are difficult people important in our lives?

    a) Because we are sadomasochists
    b) Because they take advantage of our naiveté
    c) Because they allow us to practice with them the tools that Love supplies us with, so that they may recognize them in their self-Love
    d) None of the above

36) The characteristics of bidirectional open communications are:

    a) Visual attention and body language must reflect openness and attention (see with the eyes of the Spirit)
    b) We mustn't allow our prejudices (individual habits) to interfere with communications
    c) Remember that no one is absolutely right all the time and allow yourselves to be wrong in order to learn from others' viewpoints
    d) All of the above

37) Compassionate Intelligence is when:

a) We are heartbroken and are very angry with injustices perpetrated by man upon other men
b) We allow others to mistreat us without avenging ourselves, even though we are itching to do so inside
c) We learn to look at every being with the eyes of the Spirit (heart)
d) None of the above

38) What does the return to the Garden of Eden mean?

a) It's an act of re-encountering our two natures (reconciliation, connection or communion)
b) It's an act of learning to see the universe anew without judgments and preconceptions (looking with the eyes of the spirit)
c) It's an act of forgiveness towards ourselves and others
d) All of the above

39) Why is forgiveness the most efficient way of demonstrating Love in the universe?

a) Because when you forgive the actions of those who know not what they do, we remove the need for suffering that the law of Love seeks in their lives
b) Because forgiveness bounces with an amplified force and heals all of the ignorant mistakes in my self
c) Because "just as you do for smallest of my brothers, you do unto me"
d) All of the above

BIBLIOGRAPHY OF BOOKS THAT HELPED ME CREATE MY VISION, DIRECTLY OR INDIRECTLY

1. The Bible
2. Khenchen Palden Sherab Rinpoche. *Door To Inconceivable Wisdom and Compassion.*
3. Kenchen Palden Sherab Rinpoche *Opening to Our Primordial Nature.*
4. Lao-Tzu. *Tao Te Ching.*
5. Rabi Shimon bar Yojai. *El Zohar.*
6. The Three Initiates. *El Kybalion.*
7. Paramahansa Yogananda. *Autobiography of a Yogi.*
8. Plato. *Dialogues.*
9. Amit Goswami Ph.D. *The Self-Aware Universe.*
10. Ken Wilder. *A Brief History of everything.*
11. Chogyam Trungpa. *Cutting Through Spiritual Materialism.*
12. M. Scott Peck. *The Road Less Traveled.*
13. Hermann Hesse. *Siddhartha.*
14. Shantideva. *The Guide to the Bodhisattva Way Of Life.*
15. Sogyal Rinpoche. *The Tibetan Book of Living and Dying.*
16. Jerry Jampolsky. *Love Is Letting Go of Fear.*
17. Richard Bach. *Illusions.*
18. Helen Schucman. *A Course in Miracles.*
19. Deepak Chopra. *Quantum Healing.*
20. Khalil Gibran. *The Prophet.*
21. Franca Canónico. *El Ser Uno* (6 volúmenes). www. elseruno.com

Iván Figueroa Otero M.D. FACS, FAAMA

After graduating from the School of Medicine of the University of PR, Dr. Figueroa Otero trains as General Surgeon at the University Hospital of the UPR, integrating a one-year fellowship in the study of cancer, and one in experimental research and clinic. Post-graduate studies in Pediatric Surgery at Miami Children's Hospital and the Hospital of San Juan Municipal Hospital followed.

Looking for non-surgical or less invasive options for pediatric conditions, Dr. Figueroa Otero explores Eastern philosophies that emphasize a holistic concept. He was one of the first physicians to become certified in medical acupuncture in Puerto Rico, training in traditional Chinese medicine and acupuncture with professors from the University of Seville. Eventually he was certified in medical acupuncture nationwide.

In 2009, the Dr. got a certification in anti- aging medicine and in December of that year he retired from the practice of pediatric surgery, focusing instead on a comprehensive medical practice and emphasizing disease prevention and modifying styles life. In 2011 he was invited to become a Trustee of the American Board of Medical Acupuncture, which is the national body responsible for certifying physicians in the field of acupuncture through national exams. In that same year he was recognized by Natural Awakenings Magazine as *Holistic Physician of the Year.*

Dr. Figueroa Otero is currently engaged in his private practice and continues in his role as an educator, trying to achieve full integration of traditional Chinese acupuncture courses in the curriculum of medical schools, allowing the physicians to be certified both locally and nationally, and to establish clinical research protocols on the use of acupuncture in known conditions compared to the methodology established by modern medicine. Another immediate priority is to incorporate meditation techniques and their role in preventive and therapeutic medicine.

Printed in the United States
By Bookmasters